All Our Children

By Stephen Unwin

All Our Children was first produced by Tara Finney Productions
in association with Jermyn Street Theatre, receiving its world
premiere at Jermyn Street Theatre, London, on 26 April 2017.

All Our Children

By Stephen Unwin

CAST

Eric	Edward Franklin
Martha	Rebecca Johnson
Elizabetta	Lucy Speed
Victor	Colin Tierney
Bishop von Galen	David Yelland

CREATIVE TEAM

Director	Stephen Unwin
Designer	Simon Higlett
Lighting Designer	Tim Mascall
Sound Designer	John Leonard
Casting Director	Ginny Schiller CDG
Associate Director	Nathan Markiewicz
Costume Supervisor	Karen Large
Casting Assistant	Amy Beadel

PRODUCTION TEAM

Producer	Tara Finney Productions in association with Jermyn Street Theatre
Production Manager	Ben Karakashian
Stage Manager	Lisa Cochrane
Press Representative	Clióna Roberts CRPR
Marketing	JHI Marketing
Graphic Design	Rebecca Pitt

SUPPORTERS AND THANKS

All Our Children would not have been possible without the support of:

The Leche Trust
Royce Bell
The Michelle Cuttler and John Van de North Family
Anna Fleming & Richard Stokes
Jimm Cox
Yogi & Erin Hiremath
Thomas Grant QC
Jill Segal

We would also like to thank:

Jerwood Foundation
Chichester Festival Theatre
Angels Costumes
Young Vic
Rose Theatre Kingston
Paul Warmsley
Kevin McCurdy
Jermyn Street Theatre Technical Team
Anthony, Penny & all at Jermyn Street Theatre

KIDS

The production is proud to support the work of KIDS.

KIDS is a national charity, founded over 47 years ago, providing a wide range of support services to disabled children, young people and their families. We support children with any disability from birth to 25 years of age. We offer our support to the whole family with the aim of giving disabled children a brighter future.

We cannot change a diagnosis and we cannot cure but we can, and we do, make a very real difference to the lives of families with a disabled child, through high-quality, practical and tailored services delivered by dedicated professional staff. KIDS provides over 120 different services and works with 80 local authorities throughout England.

We are passionate about making a life-changing, positive difference to the lives of disabled children and young people and their families.

For more information, please visit: **www.kids.org.uk**

CAST

EDWARD FRANKLIN | ERIC

Theatre credits include: *The Importance of Being Earnest* (Birmingham Rep); *Hay Fever* (Theatre Royal Bath/UK and Australian tour/Duke of York's); *Shakespeare in Love* (Noël Coward); *Twelve Angry Men* (Birmingham Rep/Garrick); *Dances of Death, Wittenberg* (Gate); *The Merchant of Venice* (Creation Theatre Company); *How to Think the Unthinkable* (Unicorn); *Punk Rock* (UK tour).

Television credits include: *Doctor Thorne, Doctors, Being Human, Married, Single, Other.*

Film credits include: *Denial, Home, The Brain Hack.*

REBECCA JOHNSON | MARTHA

Theatre credits include: *Present Laughter, This Happy Breed* (Theatre Royal Bath); *A Day in the Death of Joe Egg* (Liverpool Playhouse/Rose Theatre Kingston); *The Way of the World, The Importance of Being Earnest* (Chichester Festival Theatre); *Wendy & Peter Pan, The Dog in the Manger, Tamar's Revenge, The House of Desires, Pedro the Great Pretender* (RSC); *Coram Boy, Mourning Becomes Electra, Edmond, Peter Pan* (National Theatre); *Twelfth Night, The Comedy of Errors, What the Butler Saw, Macbeth* (Sheffield Theatres); *As You Like It, Love's Labour's Lost, A Midsummer Night's Dream, Troilus and Cressida* (Regent's Park Open Air Theatre); *The Front Page* (Donmar Warehouse).

Television credits include: *The Trip to Spain, Anna Mann's Valentine, Suspects, The Trip to Italy, The Trip, Dark Matters, Holby City, Five Daughters, Casualty 1909, Casualty 1907, Casualty 1906, Beau Brummell, Midsomer Murders, Foyle's War, The Royal, Spooks, Gentlemen's Relish, Poirot, Frank Stubbs Promotes, Just William, Jonathan Creek.*

Film credits include: *Harbour, The Listener, The Carrier, Hedda, Shackleton, Two Seconds to Midnight.*

LUCY SPEED | ELIZABETTA

Theatre credits include: *Rosie Blitz* (Polka); *Twelfth Night* (Royal & Derngate); *The Vagina Monologues* (Wyndham's); *Be My Baby* (Soho); *Twelfth Night/See How they Run, Girls Night* (UK tour); *Price of Meat* (Nuffield Southampton); *Amateur Girl* (St. James Theatre/Nottingham Playhouse); *Neaptide* (National Theatre).

Television credits include: *Jamie Johnson, Cradle to Grave, National Treasure, Call the Midwife, Love Soup, Men Behaving Badly, The Bill, Dangerfield, Unsuitable Job for a Woman, Jericho, The Prince and the Pauper, Saracen, Lewis, Law and Order, EastEnders, Holby City, The Dumping Ground.*

Film credits include: *Impromptu, Scoop, England My England, Metroland, Keep The Aspidistra Flying, Shakespeare in Love.*

COLIN TIERNEY | VICTOR

Theatre credits include: *The Odyssey* (Liverpool Everyman/Shakespeare's Globe); *The Father* (Theatre Royal Bath/Tricycle); *Paul, Othello, Guiding Star, The Machine Wreckers* (National Theatre); *The Duchess of Malfi, Henry VI* (RSC); *The Last Days of Troy, The Seagull, Cold Meat Party, Britannia Waves the Rules* (Royal Exchange Manchester); *The Misanthrope, Tartuffe* (Liverpool Playhouse/ETT); *Betrayal, Hamlet* (Sheffield Crucible); *Hedda Gabler* (Theatre Royal Bath/UK tour); *How Love is Spelt* (Bush); *Death of Cool* (Hampstead); *Ivanov, The Life of Galileo* (Almeida); *Hamlet* (Bristol Old Vic).

Television credits include: *Lucky Man, Vera, Silent Witness, DCI Banks, Garrow's Law, New Tricks, Inspector Lynley, The Walk, Island at War, The Vice, Tough Love, Midsomer Murders.*

Film credits include: *Nowhere Boy, Splintered, Bye Bye Baby.*

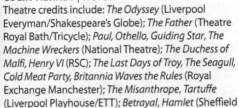

DAVID YELLAND | BISHOP VON GALEN

Theatre credits include: *The Winter's Tale* (Shakespeare's Globe); *Taken at Midnight* (Haymarket); *An Ideal Husband, Mrs Warren's Profession* (Gate, Dublin); *A Marvellous Year for Plum, The Circle* (Chichester Festival Theatre); *Uncle Vanya* (Print Room); *Henry IV* (Peter Hall Company, Theatre Royal, Bath); *Mrs Warren's Profession* (Comedy); *Nicholas Nickleby* (Gielgud/Toronto).

Television credits include: *Endeavour, Midsomer Murders, Father Brown, The Crown, Reg, Midsomer Murders, Poirot, Foyle's War, Bones, Waking the Dead, Law and Order UK.*

Film credits include: *Happy End, Private Peaceful, Coriolanus, Chariots of Fire.*

CREATIVES

STEPHEN UNWIN | WRITER & DIRECTOR
Stephen Unwin is one of the UK's leading theatre and opera directors. He founded the English Touring Theatre in 1993 and opened the Rose Theatre Kingston in 2008 becoming Artistic Director until 2014.

All Our Children is Unwin's first original play, although he has written eight books on theatre and drama and translated several plays. Stephen is a campaigner for the rights and opportunities of people with learning disabilities and was appointed the Chair of KIDS in November 2016, the national charity providing services to disabled children, young people and their families.

SIMON HIGLETT | DESIGNER
Recent design credits include: *Much Ado About Nothing, Love's Labour's Lost* (Theatre Royal Haymarket); *The Marriage of Figaro* (Scottish Opera); *Big The Musical* (UK tour); *Hobson's Choice* (West End); *Present Laughter* (Theatre Royal Bath); *Chitty Chitty Bang Bang* (West Yorkshire Playhouse/ UK tour); *Singin' in the Rain* (West End/Chichester Festival Theatre/ international tour); *Blithe Spirit* (West End/US tour); *Derren Brown's Miracle* (West End/UK tour); *The Importance of Being Ernest* (Washington DC); *Mrs Pat, Amadeus, An Ideal Husband, Stevie* (Chichester Festival Theatre); *Saturday Night Fever* (Denmark).

Other theatre credits include: *The Magic Flute* (Scottish Opera); *The Resistible Rise of Arturo Ui, Yes Prime Minister, Rosencrantz and Guildenstern Are Dead, When We Are Married, The Rivals, Man and Boy, Hay Fever, Amy's View* (West End); *Enemies, Whistling Psyche, The Earthly Paradise* (Almeida); *The Accidental Death of an Anarchist* (Donmar Warehouse); *The Force of Change* (Royal Court); *The Merry Wives of Windsor* (Stockholm); *An Ideal Husband, Mrs Warren's Profession* (Washington DC); *Haunted* (Brits Off Broadway, New York); *Pygmalion* (Old Vic); *Singer, Thomas More* (RSC); *The Brothers Karamzov* (Manchester Royal Exchange); *To Kill a Mockingbird* (West Yorkshire Playhouse); *Of Mice and Men* (Birmingham Rep).

TIM MASCALL | LIGHTING DESIGNER

Theatre credits include: *Jumpy, A Taste of Honey, Long Day's Journey into Night, Kill Jonny Glendenning, Faith Healer* (Royal Lyceum, Edinburgh); *Licensed to Ill* (Cornershop); *The Truth, A Little Night Music, My Fair Lady, Who's Afraid of Virginia Woolf?*(Central Theatre, Budapest); *I Have Been Here Before, Bloody Poetry, The Autumn Garden, The Notorious Mrs Ebbsmith* (Jermyn Street); *Without You, Breakfast with Jonny Wilkinson, Fully Committed* (Menier Chocolate Factory); *Why the Whales Came* (Harold Pinter); *The Vagina Monologues* (Wyndham's); *Eric and Little Ern, Potted Panto* (Vaudeville); *Invincible* (St. James Theatre); *Derren Brown's Miracle, Infamous* (Palace); *Something Wicked This Way Comes* (Old Vic); *Enigma* (Adelphi); *Evening of Wonder, Potted Potter* (Garrick); *Ruby Wax: Losing It* (Duchess).

Opera credits include: *Peter Grimes, The Gamblers* (LPO at the Royal Festival Hall); *Aida* (Opera Holland Park); *The Cunning Little Vixen* (Garsington).

JOHN LEONARD | SOUND DESIGNER

John started work in theatre sound over forty years ago and during that time has provided soundtracks for theatres all over the world. Author of an acclaimed guide to theatre sound, he is the recipient of multiple awards, a Fellow of the Guildhall School of Music & Drama and an Honorary Fellow of the Hong Kong Academy of Performing Arts.

Recent sound design credits include: *One Night in Miami* (Donmar Warehouse); *The Libertine* (Theatre Royal Bath/West End); *Macbeth* (Shakespeare's Globe); *Long Day's Journey into Night* (Bristol Old Vic); *Firebird* (Hampstead/Trafalgar); *Little Eyolf* (Almeida); *Waste* (National Theatre); *Mr Foote's Other Leg* (Hampstead/West End); *Ghosts* (Almeida/West End/New York).

Other credits include: *Birthday, Tribes* (Royal Court); *The Heresy of Love* (RSC); *The Deep Blue Sea* (Chichester Festival Theatre); *The Master Builder, The Dark Earth, The Light Sky* (Almeida); *London Assurance* (National Theatre).

GINNY SCHILLER CDG | CASTING DIRECTOR
Ginny has been in-house casting director for the Royal Shakespeare
Company, Chichester Festival Theatre, Rose Theatre Kingston, English
Touring Theatre and Soho Theatre, and is the current casting director for
the Ustinov Theatre, Bath, under the Artistic Directorship of Laurence
Boswell. She has worked on many shows for the West End and No. 1
touring circuit as well as for the Almeida, Arcola, Bath Theatre Royal,
Birmingham Rep, Bolton Octagon, Bristol Old Vic, Clwyd Theatr Cymru,
Frantic Assembly, Greenwich Theatre, Hampstead Theatre, Headlong,
Liverpool Everyman and Playhouse, Lyric Theatre Belfast, Menier
Chocolate Factory, Norfolk & Norwich Festival, Northampton Royal &
Derngate, Oxford Playhouse, Plymouth Theatre Royal and Drum, Regent's
Park Open Air Theatre, Shared Experience, Sheffield Crucible, West
Yorkshire Playhouse, Wilton's Music Hall and Young Vic. She has also
worked on many television, film and radio productions.

NATHAN MARKIEWICZ | ASSOCIATE DIRECTOR
Directing credits include: *Creditors* (Warren Wilson); *The Fix* (Camden
Fringe Festival); *Stella Europa* (Hen & Chicken's).

Assisting credits include: *A View from the Bridge* (UK tour).

KAREN LARGE | COSTUME SUPERVISOR
Recent credits include: *Love Labour's Lost, Much Ado About Nothing*
(Chichester Festival Theatre/Theatre Royal Haymarket); *Platonov, Ivanov,
Seagull* (National Theatre/Chichester Festival Theatre); *Travels with My
Aunt, Mrs Pat, Educating Rita, An Ideal Husband, Amadeus, The Way of the
World* (Chichester Festival Theatre); *West Side Story* (Kilworth House);
Hobson's Choice (Theatre Royal Bath/Vaudeville); *She Stoops to Conquer,
Who's Afraid of Virginia Woolf?* (Theatre Royal Bath); *The Producers* (UK
tour); *Annie Get Your Gun* (UK tour); *Candide, Travels with My Aunt,
Charley's Aunt* (Menier Chocolate Factory); *Macbeth* (Shakespeare's
Globe); *The Promise* (Trafalgar Studios); *Top Girls, Big Fella, Anderson's
English, Tea with Doctor Johnson* (Out of Joint).

BEN KARAKASHIAN | PRODUCTION MANAGER

Ben graduated from Royal Holloway University of London with a BA Honors in Drama and Theatre Studies.

Production management credits include: *The Plague, New Nigerians, Kenny Morgan, The Divided Laing* (Arcola); *Death Takes a Holiday, Ragtime, Titanic the Musical, In the Bar of a Tokyo Hotel, The Mikado* (Charing Cross); *Frontier Trilogy* (Rabenhof Theatre, Vienna/Edinburgh Fringe Festival); *Home Chat* (Finborough); *The Man Who Shot Liberty Valance* (Park); *Our Ajax* (Southwark Playhouse); *The Bunker Trilogy* (Southwark Playhouse/ Seoul Performing Arts Festival/Stratford Circus).

Stage management credits includes: *Our Ajax, Moment of Truth, Tanzi Libre, Feathers in the Snow* (Southwark Playhouse); *Black Jesus, Soft of Her Palm, The Grand Duke, Goodnight Bird, Portraits, Perchance to Dream* (Finborough); *Someone to Blame* (King's Head).

LISA COCHRANE | STAGE MANAGER

Lisa trained in Professional Production Skills at Guildford School of Acting.

Recent theatre credits include: ASM *All My Sons* (Rose Theatre Kingston/ Hong Kong); DSM *Aladdin* (Blackpool Grand); SM on Book *The Acedian Pirates* (Theatre503); ASM *Encounters with the Past* (Hampton Court Palace); ASM *Le Nozze di Figaro, Alcina* (Longborough Festival Opera); SM on Book *My Mother Said I Never Should* (St. James Theatre); SM on Book *Land of Our Fathers* (UK tour/Found111); DSM *Peter Pan* (Malvern Theatres); SM on Book *And Then Come the Nightjars* (Theatre503/Bristol Old Vic); ASM *Don Pasquale, Rigoletto* (Longborough Festival Opera); DSM *A Matter of Life & Death* (Electric Theatre Guildford); SM *WINK* (Theatre503); DSM *Sleeping Beauty* (Blackpool Grand); SM on Book *Land of Our Fathers* (Trafalgar Studios).

Tara Finney Productions Ltd

Tara Finney Productions was set up to produce the critically acclaimed *Land of Our Fathers* which was Time Out's *Fringe Show of the Year* when it premiered in September 2013. In March 2015, she produced *WINK* starring *Harry Potter and the Cursed Child* star Sam Clemmett.

In 2016, TFP presented the national tour of *And Then Come The Nightjars* in collaboration with Theatre503 and Bristol Old Vic, the world premiere of Theatre503 Playwriting Award finalist *The Acedian Pirates* and acted as general manager for Interval Productions' new musical *MUTED* in the Bunker Theatre's inaugural season.

In early 2017, TFP produced the world premiere of Arinzé Kene's play *good dog* for tiata fahodzi and Watford Palace Theatre.

Theatre credits include:

- *good dog (*national tour)

- *MUTED* (Bunker Theatre); nominated for Off West End Awards 2017 *Best New Musical* (finalist)

- *The Acedian Pirates* (Theatre503); shortlisted for Theatre503 Playwrighting Award 2014

- *And Then Come The Nightjars* (national tour); nominated for UK Theatre Award 2016 *Best Design*, shortlisted Susan Smith Blackburn Award 2015, winner Theatre503 Playwriting Award 2014

- *WINK* (Theatre503); nominated for Off West End Awards 2015 *Best New Play*, *Most Promising Playwright*, *Best Director*, *Best Sound Designer*

- *Land of Our Fathers* (Found111/national tour/Trafalgar Studios/ Theatre503); nominated for Off West End Awards 2014 *Best New Play*, *Best Production* (finalist), *Best Director*, *Best Set Designer*, *Best Lighting Designer*

www.tarafinney.com
@tara_finney
facebook.com/tarafinneyproductions
instagram.com/tarafinneyproductions

TARA FINNEY | PRODUCER

Tara qualified as a corporate solicitor before starting her theatrical career as Resident Assistant Producer at Theatre503 in May 2012. She then worked as Producer for Iris Theatre and as Associate Producer at Company of Angels, before going freelance in July 2015. Tara also runs production company Tiny Fires with director Paul Robinson, and their inaugural production *My Mother Said I Never Should*, starring Maureen Lipman and Katie Brayben, received critical acclaim during its run at St. James Theatre in spring 2016 – www.tinyfires.co.uk. Tara is supported by Stage One.

Other theatre credits include: *World Factory* (Young Vic/New Wolsey); Theatre Café Woolwich (Greenwich & Lewisham Young People's Theatre); *Helver's Night* (York Theatre Royal); *Alice Through the Looking Glass, Richard III* (St Paul's Church); *Respect, Buy Nothing Day* (ALRA Studio); *I, Peaseblossom / I, Caliban* (national tour); Theatre Café York (York Theatre Royal); *Alice in Wonderland, Julius Caesar* (St Paul's Church); *Desolate Heaven, Where the Mangrove Grows, ELEGY, Life for Beginners* (Theatre503); *Bluebird* (Bedlam/Courtyard/South Hill Park).

ELLIE CLAUGHTON | ASSISTANT PRODUCER

Ellie is a freelance theatre producer working in London and across the UK. She is currently working as a producer for LUNG Theatre, Changing Face, She Productions and Plane Paper Theatre.

Her recent projects include: *E15* (BAC/UK tour); *The Pulverised* (Arcola/York Theatre Royal); *It Is So Ordered* (Pleasance); *Dreamless Sleep* (Upstairs at the Arts); *The StorytEllas* (East Riding Theatre); *Odd Shaped Balls* (Old Red Lion); *Don't Smoke in Bed* (Finborough).

JERMYN STREET THEATRE

During the 1930s the basement of 16b Jermyn Street was home to the glamorous Monseigneur Restaurant and Club. The space was converted into a theatre by Howard Jameson and Penny Horner in the early 1990s, and Jermyn Street Theatre staged its first production in August 1994. Over the last twenty years the theatre has established itself as one of London's leading Off-West End studio theatres.

Gene David Kirk became Artistic Director in 2009. With his Associate Director Anthony Biggs he was instrumental in transforming the theatre's creative output with critically acclaimed revivals of rarely performed plays including Charles Morgan's post-war classic *The River Line*, the UK premiere of Ibsen's first performed play *St John's Night* with Olivier-winning actress Sarah Crowe, and another Ibsen, his rarely performed late play *Little Eyolf* starring Imogen Stubbs and Doreen Mantle.

Other notable successes include seventies musical *Boy Meets Boy*, which was nominated for six Off West End Awards, *The Two Character Play* by Tennessee Williams, Graham Greene's *The Living Room* and the Ivor Novello musical *Gay's the Word*. In 2012, Trevor Nunn directed the world premiere of Samuel Beckett's radio play *All That Fall* starring Eileen Atkins and Michael Gambon. The production subsequently transferred to the West End's Arts Theatre and then to New York's 59E59 Theatre.

Anthony Biggs became Artistic Director in 2013 and has continued the policy of staging rediscovered classic plays alongside new plays and musicals, with a renewed focus on emerging artists and writers from outside the UK. Recent revivals include Eugene O'Neill's early American work *The First Man*, John Van Druten's First World War drama *Flowers of the Forest*, and South African Reza de Wet's supernatural tale *Fever*. New work includes US playwright Ruby Rae Spiegel's exploration of teenage sexuality *Dry Land*, Jonathan Lewis's anarchic comedy about young people in the education system *A Level Playing Field*, and Sarah Daniels' *Soldiers' Wives* starring Cath Shipton, a stage adaptation of Sarah's acclaimed BBC Radio play about five women living on a British army base whose husbands are serving in Afghanistan.

Jermyn Street Theatre was nominated for the Peter Brook Empty Space Award in 2011 and won the Stage 100 Best Fringe Theatre in 2012.

Jermyn Street Theatre is a registered charity and receives no public subsidy.

ALL OUR CHILDREN

Stephen Unwin

'The unexamined life is not worth living.'

Socrates

'Lives Unworthy of Life'

The persecution, sterilisation and murder of hundreds of thousands of disabled people is one of the most overlooked chapters in the whole ghastly history of Nazi Germany.

Between 1939 and 1941 as many as 100,000 people with a wide range of disabilities were dismissed as *lebensunwertes Leben* ('lives unworthy of life') and systematically killed in six converted psychiatric hospitals across Austria and Germany. Initially, lethal injections were used but soon, at Hitler's personal recommendation, carbon monoxide was employed.

Aktion T4, as the programme was called, was a logical extension of the eugenics movement, which had attracted support from a wide range of people, many with impeccable liberal credentials, across Europe and the United States. Few had suggested murder (although Virginia Woolf, confronted by a group of 'imbeciles', wrote in 1915 that 'they should certainly be killed'), but the Nazi programme of compulsory sterilisation of people with 'congenital conditions' was widely accepted.

With the outbreak of war, the persecution escalated dramatically and, on September 1st, 1939 (the day of the invasion of Poland), Hitler signed his notorious Euthanasia Decree which stated that, 'after a discerning diagnosis', 'incurable patients' should be 'granted mercy death'. Intellectually justified by Social Darwinism, this policy received popular support on the grounds of cost, with a poster claiming that a man 'suffering from a hereditary defect cost "the People's Community" 60,000 Reichmarks during his lifetime'. As a leading Nazi doctor said, 'the idea is unbearable to me that the best, the flower of our youth, must lose its life at the front in order that feebleminded and irresponsible asocial elements can have a secure existence in the asylum.'

By early 1941, 5,000 children, many only a few months old, with a wide range of conditions – Down syndrome, 'idiocy', cerebral palsy, and so on – had been assessed, registered and murdered. Initially, their parents were asked for their consent and a panel of three 'medical experts' was convened to agree on the course of action. In due course, however, deception and social pressure were deployed, and children were sent to so-called 'special sections', apparently to receive medical treatment, but instead bussed off to their deaths.

Public opposition to the programme was limited. Probably the most striking intervention came from the churches, especially the Catholic Bishop of Münster. Clemens August Graf von Galen (1878–1946) belonged to one of the oldest aristocratic families in Germany. He spent twenty-three years (1906–29) working as a parish priest in a poor district in Berlin but, as a staunch conservative, had opposed what he perceived to be the immorality of the Weimar Republic. Indeed, the Nazis, who saw him as an ally, welcomed his installation as Bishop of Münster in 1933. From the outset, however, he objected to many aspects of the regime, and took editorial responsibility for a volume of essays criticising the paganism of the philosopher and ideologue Alfred Rosenberg. He voiced his disapproval of Nazi racial theories and helped draft Pope Pius XI's anti-Nazi encyclical *Mit brennender Sorge* (1937).

He is best known, however, for his criticism of the murder of the disabled and, in July and August 1941, delivered three sermons which didn't just criticise the programme: they challenged the entire Nazi value system. In one of them he asked why these 'unproductive citizens' were killed:

The opinion is that since they can no longer make money, they are obsolete machines, comparable with some old cow that can no longer give milk or some horse that has gone lame. What is the lot of unproductive machines and cattle? They are destroyed. I have no intention of stretching this comparison further. The case here is not one of machines or cattle which exist to serve men and furnish them with plenty. They may be legitimately done away with when they can no longer fulfill their function. Here we are dealing with human beings, with our neighbours, brothers and sisters, the poor and invalids... unproductive – perhaps! But have they, therefore, lost the right to live? Have you or I the right to exist only because we are 'productive'? If the principle is established that unproductive human beings may be killed, then God help all those invalids who, in order to produce wealth, have given their all and sacrificed their strength of body. If all unproductive people may thus be violently eliminated, then woe betide our brave soldiers who return home, wounded, maimed or sick.

Thousands of copies of the sermons were illegally circulated and local protest groups broke the silence that surrounded the programme. Copies were also dropped by the RAF and inspired various resistance groups.

The Nazis were in two minds about how to respond to the 'Lion of Münster'. Some advised Hitler to execute von Galen or, at least, send him to a concentration camp; but others, especially Goebbels and Bormann, recognised the danger of alienating German Catholics, and von Galen – a close friend of the new Pope, Pius XII – was subjected to house arrest from late 1941 onwards. Hitler declared ominously in a private conversation that 'the fact that I remain silent in public over Church affairs is not in the least misunderstood by the sly foxes of the Catholic Church, and I am quite sure that a man like Bishop von Galen knows full well that after the war I shall extract retribution to the last farthing'. Von Galen survived Hitler, dying of natural causes in 1946, and was beatified by his fellow German, Pope Benedict XVI, in 2005.

Astonishingly, partly as a result of von Galen's intervention, the programme was formally discontinued in August 1941. It would be overstating the case to say that he stopped the murder (a further 100,000 disabled people were killed before the end of the war in less formal settings), and many of the techniques and personnel were employed in the far greater Jewish Holocaust that escalated so dramatically after 1941. Nevertheless, his denunciation was one of the most courageous and outspoken acts of resistance in Third Reich.

All Our Children is very much a work of fiction. There is no evidence that von Galen had a meeting of the kind that I have dramatised (though he did talk with senior figures in the SS) nor do we know of a doctor involved in the programme having qualms about what he was doing. What's clear, however, is that his intervention raised the most profound questions about the innate value of the human being, regardless of cost or productivity, and his voice, for all its stubborn absolutism, deserves to be heard.

It would be absurd to claim that disabled children face anything like this level of discrimination today. Nevertheless, there is a huge amount to be done to ensure that they're given the same opportunities as their able-bodied siblings. It's often said that you can judge a society by the way that it treats its most vulnerable. If Nazi Germany failed that test in the most abject way imaginable, we should never forget its terrible lessons.

Stephen Unwin,
London, 2017

A reading of an earlier draft was held at English Touring Theatre on 23rd September 2014, under the title of *T4*, with the following cast:

VICTOR	Guy Henry
MARTHA	Lucy Briers
ERIC	David Dawson
ELIZABETTA	Kelly Hunter
BISHOP VON GALEN	Simon Russell Beale

Dog Fox Field

The test for feeblemindedness was, they had to make up a
sentence using the words 'dog', 'fox' and 'field'.

'Judgement at Nuremberg'

These were no leaders, but they were first
into the dark on Dog Fox Field:

Anna who rocked her head, and Paul
who grew big and yet giggled small,

Irma who looked Chinese, and Hans
who knew his world as a fox knows a field.

Hunted with needles, exposed, unfed,
this time in their thousands they bore sad cuts

for having gazed, and shuffled, and failed
to field the lore of prey and hound

they then had to thump and cry in the vans
that ran while stopped in Dog Fox Field.

Our sentries, whose holocaust does not end,
they show us when we cross into Dog Fox Field.

Les Murray

To Joey

Characters

VICTOR FRANZ, *a doctor, Director of the Clinic*
MARTHA, *a maid*
ERIC, *Deputy Director, Administrator*
ELIZABETTA, *a mother*
BISHOP VON GALEN

Setting

Winkelheim, 6 January 1941

Music

Winterreise, Franz Schubert

This text went to press before the end of rehearsals and so may differ slightly from the play as performed.

ACT ONE

VICTOR*'s office. Dawn.*

On one side, a large desk, window behind it. Heavy curtains.
On the other, two comfortable chairs and a small round table
beside a stove. One double door into the room. There is a wall
with a large number of box files. Medical certificates. A painting.
Comfortable fittings. Radio and phone on his desk.

VICTOR *is asleep by the stove. The curtains are shut. The stove*
has burnt out. The room is dark.

MARTHA *comes in. She doesn't see* VICTOR *at first. She goes*
over to put some letters on VICTOR*'s desk, and opens the*
curtains. Brilliant winter sunlight floods in. She turns and is
very surprised to see him.

MARTHA. Oh, Doctor, you gave me such a shock.

VICTOR. I'm sorry, I must have –

MARTHA. Haven't you been back to your room?

VICTOR. Herr Schmidt and I had a chat last night, and I never
managed to –

MARTHA. Let me clear that up.

She clears up the remnants of sandwiches and beer from
the table.

VICTOR. Good beer, by the way, Martha.

MARTHA. Not much of that cognac left, I see.

VICTOR. It was mostly me, I'm afraid. Herr Schmidt didn't
stay long. And I sat here reading and –

MARTHA. Fell asleep?

VICTOR. Yes.

MARTHA. You should sleep in your own bed, Doctor, or you'll
get ill. Then where would we be?

VICTOR. Indeed.

Coughs.

MARTHA. It's terribly cold this morning. I slipped on the ice. Bit of a bruise, actually, here.

VICTOR. You be careful, Martha. I've got some cream somewhere for –

MARTHA. Oh don't you worry. I'll get you your breakfast.

VICTOR. And some water, I think, so I can wash my face.

MARTHA (*smiles*). Righty-ho.

Leaves. There is a pause. VICTOR *picks up a box file at his feet, and glances at a page.*

VICTOR. Oh Christ.

Closes the file and takes it over to the bookcase. MARTHA *returns with a jug of water and a towel.*

Thank you.

She goes. He takes off his shirt and washes himself. She returns.

That's better. Healthy mind in a healthy body.

He dries himself.

Thank you.

He starts to cough.

MARTHA. Oh dear: that cough of yours. It's not getting better, is it?

She leaves.

VICTOR *does a few stretching exercises and puts the new shirt on. Turns the radio on. German news.* VICTOR *impatiently retunes it. Classical music. He stares out the window for a moment.* MARTHA *returns with breakfast: coffee, bread, ham and cheese.*

Here we are. Breakfast.

He turns the radio off and sits at the table as MARTHA *lays out his breakfast.*

VICTOR (*about the coffee*). Is it real?

MARTHA (*laughs*). Herr Schmidt got hold of some beans. God knows where from.

VICTOR. Mmm, good. He's clever, our Eric. With a drop of that cognac, I think, don't you?

MARTHA (*smiling*). Well, you're the doctor...

She takes the coffee to the drinks table and drains the bottle.

That's the end of it, I'm afraid.

Hands it back to him. He sips it.

VICTOR. Lovely.

MARTHA. Cheese?

VICTOR. Oh yes.

Tastes it.

Dutch?

MARTHA *smiles.*

Delicious. So, Martha, how's everything? Family all right?

MARTHA. Not bad, thank you. Hans had a week away, camping. Training, really. Long hikes and too much beer as far as I can tell. And Grete's been on a course with the BDM. Cooking, cleaning, that sort of thing.

VICTOR. Perfect for a teenage girl. How old is she now?

MARTHA. Seventeen last October.

VICTOR. Really? I remember her coming here –

MARTHA. I know. Feels like last week.

VICTOR. Has she got a boyfriend yet?

MARTHA. Oh, don't be silly. She's much too young.

VICTOR. Yes, but, hearth and home, you know.

MARTHA. Oh, she'll marry when the time is right.

VICTOR. And how's Freddy's chest? You were worried.

MARTHA. Nothing serious, thank God. He just can't shake it off.

VICTOR. Well, this weather. Forecast says it's going to snow. You should take him to a doctor.

They look at each other.

Not me, obviously.

They both laugh.

MARTHA. No.

VICTOR. I wouldn't mind seeing some normal children again. I used to, remember?

MARTHA. Before.

VICTOR. The old days, eh?

Pause.

Not like this lot now. More's the pity.

MARTHA. Freddy's very normal, thank heavens, just perfect.

VICTOR. I'm sure.

MARTHA. Never stops talking. Amazing, for a five-year-old, so his teacher says. A right little chatterbox. Friedrich is special, is what I think.

VICTOR. Do they miss their father?

MARTHA. Yes, but Christof writes now and then. Not often, but when he can.

VICTOR. And they reply?

MARTHA. Grete does. Sometimes.

VICTOR. Where's he stationed?

MARTHA. Out east, I think.

VICTOR. Poland?

MARTHA. Must be. Infantry, you know. Nothing fancy.

VICTOR. I see.

MARTHA. This was their first Christmas without him.

VICTOR. What a shame. Christmas is a time for the family, people always say.

Stands up.

Thank you, that was perfect. Well, I must get on. When Herr Schmidt gets in, ask him to come and see me, would you?

MARTHA (*clearing up the breakfast*). Of course. Oh, and I meant to say, Doctor, there's a Frau Pabst wants to see you. She's one of the mothers. I said she could come at eight, when she gets off her night shift. I hope you don't mind.

VICTOR. That's rather –

MARTHA. She just wants to thank you. She was very insistent. I'm sure she won't take long.

VICTOR. I see.

Pause.

That's a bit –

MARTHA. I know. I'm sorry. I couldn't say no –

VICTOR. Well, if I have to.

MARTHA. It would be a kindness. I feel for the mothers. Imagine having one of them –

VICTOR. Very well. Thank you, Martha.

MARTHA *leaves.* VICTOR *goes to the desk and lights a cigarette, and stares out of the window. There's a pause.*

How does it go again?

(*Reciting.*) *Über allen Gipfeln*
Ist Ruh. In allen Wipfeln
Spürest du
Kaum einen Hauch –

ERIC *comes in. Suddenly.*

ERIC. Heil Hitler.

VICTOR. Ah, there you are.

ERIC. What was that you were saying just now?

VICTOR. Goethe.

ERIC. Really?

VICTOR. Our national poet, you know.

ERIC. I see.

VICTOR. The land of writers and thinkers.

ERIC. Right.

Pause.

No, I don't know what you're talking about, I'm sorry.

VICTOR. Oh, it doesn't matter.

Pause.

But look at the trees. Beautiful, aren't they? So still.

ERIC. Well, that's because there's no wind.

VICTOR. Peaceful. Don't you think?

ERIC. If you say so. It's bloody cold out there, that I do know.

VICTOR *coughs and wheezes.*

And that's not got any better, has it?

VICTOR. No.

ERIC. It's those cigarettes, isn't it? Bad for your health, Doctor. Last night you –

VICTOR. I know, I know.

ERIC. They're going to ban them soon, I hear.

VICTOR. Over my dead body.

ERIC (*laughing at the incongruity of what* VICTOR*'s saying*). Exactly. To save the nation's health, says Doctor Goebbels.

VICTOR. Well, they won't stop me. My one bit of freedom in this –

Still looking out of the window.

Just look at that crow. Hopping from twig to twig looking for a berry 'in all that ice and snow'. What a thankless task. But it's free. So free.

ERIC. Like you smoking?

VICTOR. Exactly.

Pause.

ERIC. I've never seen the point.

VICTOR. I'm sure. You don't get the point of poetry either, do you?

ERIC. No, I don't.

VICTOR. But you have vices of your own, Herr Schmidt, don't you?

ERIC. Certainly not.

VICTOR. No?

Pause. Again, looking at each other, silently.

ERIC *smiles. Finally:*

ERIC. I like motorbikes.

Pause.

I bought myself a new one last week, you know?

VICTOR. Oh yes?

ERIC. Zündapp K800. A 1937. What a beaut. Goes like the clappers.

Pause.

Second hand, of course. I couldn't afford –

VICTOR. Yes, yes, you're broke, I know.

ERIC. Well –

VICTOR. I'm sure you'll get a rise soon. You've only been here three months.

ERIC. I'd better.

VICTOR. Any other vices?

ERIC. Certainly not. What are you suggesting?

VICTOR. Oh nothing.

ERIC. Good.

Pause.

So, your maid told me –

VICTOR. Martha, you mean?

ERIC. Yes, Frau Trondheim said you stayed up all night, staring into the fire.

VICTOR. I did.

Pause.

ERIC. That's hardly –

VICTOR. What?

Pause.

ERIC. Did you sleep?

VICTOR. A bit.

ERIC. And didn't go over to your quarters?

VICTOR. What's it to do with you?

ERIC. Well, why – ?

Pause.

VICTOR. I couldn't –

Pause.

Nothing really.

Pause.

Bad dreams, that's all.

ERIC. Really?

VICTOR. Yes, all sorts of –

ERIC. About here?

VICTOR. Other things too.

ERIC. Really?

Pause.

How odd.

VICTOR. Quite normal, I'd say. In the circumstances –

ERIC. But, Doctor –

VICTOR. Yes?

ERIC. This is important work. You do know that, don't you?

VICTOR. Of course.

ERIC. Which requires dedication.

VICTOR. Herr Schmidt, please. I'm not – it's just –

ERIC. What?

Pause.

You should be sleeping like a baby.

VICTOR. Do you?

ERIC. Of course.

Pause.

Why ever not? Life is to be lived.

Pause.

VICTOR. And death is the end?

ERIC. You're not coming all Christian on me, are you?

Pause.

This is my youth. And I don't intend to waste it.

VICTOR. No.

Pause.

So who's the lucky lady?

ERIC. I beg your pardon?

VICTOR. Try to be a gentleman, Herr Schmidt. Kindness is –

ERIC. What?

Pause.

What an odd thing to say.

VICTOR. Perhaps.

Pause.

Who knows?

Starts coughing again.

So, what's the schedule today, then?

ERIC. Well, the morning's clear. Ward round at midday as usual. Then early lunch over in the canteen. A couple of suppliers I'd like you to meet.

Pause.

But first, Doctor, we'd better –

VICTOR. This month's transport?

ERIC. Yes. It's a larger group than usual.

VICTOR. I see.

ERIC. Thirty-two in total. Two buses.

VICTOR. What was last month?

ERIC. Twenty-four. It's these quotas. Berlin expects us to –

VICTOR. All ages?

ERIC. Mostly late teens. A few early twenties. Two younger ones, I think. We're bending the clinical guidelines as it is –

VICTOR. I see.

Pause.

ERIC. And tonight you've got a visitor.

VICTOR. Oh yes?

ERIC. Bishop von Galen, remember?

VICTOR. Christ, what does he want, do you think?

ERIC. Well, you saw his letter in the paper.

VICTOR. I did.

ERIC. Programme Director Brack wants us to deal with him.

VICTOR. Right.

ERIC. His wire just said to 'show him some respect'.

VICTOR. Oh yes, remember.

ERIC. I'm a bit disappointed, to be frank. I thought we'd done with that lot. I thought that was the whole point.

VICTOR. You'd think so, wouldn't you?

Pause.

So what am I going to say to him?

ERIC. I'm sure Berlin will tell you. Call them.

VICTOR. They never tell me anything.

ERIC. I'm sure they will. The usual stuff: taxpayers' money, improving sanitation, lightening the load on the medical profession, that sort of thing.

Pause.

VICTOR. Why can't the office do its own dirty work?

ERIC. I suspect they think you'd do it better.

VICTOR. What, and take the blame?

ERIC. No, no, not at all, they want it from the horse's mouth, as it were. Senior paediatrician. Medical experience, and so on. The Bishop will trust you.

VICTOR. So I'm being wheeled out as some kind of bloody expert, am I?

ERIC. Of course. Years of service.

VICTOR. I'm dreading it. I'm a doctor, not a –

ERIC. It's just PR, you know. Listening politely to the sentimental squeals of the ignorant. It'll be fine.

VICTOR *coughs into his handkerchief and looks for blood.*

Blood?

VICTOR. Occasionally.

ERIC. You should see a doctor.

VICTOR. Perhaps.

Pause.

ERIC. Yes. So, shall we go through this little list of mine, then?

VICTOR. Of course.

ERIC *takes a box file out of his case, and lifts out a pile of papers, each with its own photo, etc. These are real people. He gives* VICTOR *a typed list.*

ERIC. Two ticks, please: diagnosis and cure.

Gives VICTOR *a red pencil. Pause.*

VICTOR (*about the red pencil*). Thank you. This reminds me of my first year at medical school.

ERIC *smiles.* VICTOR *glances down the list. He checks each case study and says 'yes' as he marks them individually with two red ticks. This mustn't be hurried: there should be thirty-two sheets and each is a real person. After each one,* ERIC *adds it to his pile. At one point* VICTOR *stops.*

Not yet for young Karsten I think, don't you?

ERIC. If you say so.

VICTOR *starts again. And then stops again.*

VICTOR. No, no, not Edith Manstein. Really no.

ERIC. No?

VICTOR. I heard her singing the other day.

ERIC (*scornfully*). Hardly.

VICTOR. Moaning.

ERIC. Well, there you are then.

VICTOR. How old is she anyway?

ERIK. Here, it says, fourteen.

VICTOR. Why her now, I mean.

ERIC. Well, it's obvious.

VICTOR. Is it?

ERIC. Yes, straightforward idiocy. Read the report. She can't do the simplest –

Pause.

She won't notice, anyway.

VICTOR. Very well. Actually, no. Definitely not. Not Edith Manstein.

Marks a few more and stops again.

And no. Not him either. Absolutely not.

ERIC *takes the sheet back.* VICTOR *soon reaches the final sheet and hands it to* ERIC.

Thank you.

ERIC. That's twenty-nine. I'm sure Berlin will understand. Clinical independence, and all that. I can process them this afternoon.

And he starts putting the papers back in his case.

VICTOR. And what will your boys be telling them this time?

ERIC. Nice trip along the Rhine, we thought. Look at the castles, that sort of thing.

VICTOR. But the windows on the buses are painted out.

ERIC. They are now. Navy grey.

VICTOR. Perfect for sightseeing, eh?

ERIC. 'To protect the hardworking families of the Third Reich from unwanted and disturbing sights.'

VICTOR (*smiles wryly*). And will there be trouble?

ERIC. Oh they never suspect a thing. It's all very straightforward, very calm. Most of them wouldn't understand anyway.

VICTOR. And the families?

ERIC. We keep them away. After that incident in November.

VICTOR. Ah yes.

ERIC. Come and see for yourself, if you like.

VICTOR. I'd rather not.

Lights another cigarette. Pause. Coughs.

ERIC. You seem on edge this morning. What's up?

VICTOR. It's my nerves.

ERIC. More coffee?

Pause.

Forgive me for saying this, Doctor, and it's none of my business, but in my opinion, you need a woman.

VICTOR (*surprised*). Do I?

ERIC. Yes, go to Düsseldorf for the weekend. Stay in a nice hotel. Get away from this dump.

VICTOR. What an extraordinary idea.

ERIC. Dozens of ladies to choose from. It would cheer you up.

VICTOR. Maybe.

Pause.

I don't think so.

ERIC. Why did you never get married?

VICTOR. None of your business.

ERIC *gestures 'apologies'.*

Oh, the right one never came along. Anyway I'm –

ERIC. A loner?

VICTOR. Perhaps.

ERIC. Fussy?

VICTOR. It was hard after the war, you know. No time for all that.

ERIC. There's always time for love, Doctor.

Pause.

VICTOR. You don't know what I'm talking about, do you?

ERIC. Try me.

VICTOR. Well, how old are you?

ERIC. I was born on the 10th November 1918. I'm twenty-three.

VICTOR. A baby.

Pause.

Oh, forgive me, Herr Schmidt, I didn't mean –

ERIC. Doesn't matter.

VICTOR. But 1918? Absolute bloody chaos. Spartacus. And then the inflation. Don't suppose you remember that.

ERIC *shakes his head nonchalantly.*

Wheelbarrows full of money. Just to buy a few sausages. Not much time to find a wife, I can tell you.

Pause.

And I was studying hard. Six long years.

Pause.

Bloody chaos everywhere.

ERIC. And now look at us.

Pause.

Eh?

VICTOR. Where's next, d'you think?

ERIC. Russia?

VICTOR. You think?

ERIC. Would give Stalin a bit a shock, wouldn't it? Our ally and all that.

VICTOR. Indeed. And all of Europe at our feet. After all those years of –

Pause.

Good coffee, by the way. Where did you get it?

ERIC. That's more like it. Your country needs you. You need your country.

VICTOR. I know.

Smiles wanly.

Apologies.

ERIC. Not at all. I'd best be off.

VICTOR. And perhaps you could ask Martha to drop in for a moment?

ERIC. Certainly.

Turns.

And, Doctor, remember –

VICTOR. Yes, yes, Heil Hitler, I know. Now be off with you. I'd better make this call.

ERIC. Heil Hitler.

ERIC *leaves whistling, perhaps 'Horst-Wessel-Lied'.*

VICTOR *goes to his desk, sits down, looks up a number in a little directory and dials. Mutters as he's waiting for a reply:*

VICTOR. Bloody – (*Coughs. He was going to say 'fanatic'.*)

(*To the phone.*) Good morning, Franz here. Doctor Victor Franz. The Winkelheim Clinic.

Pause.

Yes, could you put me through to Herr Braun please? Thank you. Yes, Heil Hitler.

Pause.

Braun? It's Franz here. Victor Franz. Yes, how are you, Helmut?

Pause.

How many years is it now?

Pause.

Goodness.

Pause.

Yes, well I'm pleased, you've done very well. Congratulations.

Pause.

Ursula Kipper?

Pause.

Two boys and two girls? Splendid.

Pause.

No, never. No children.

Laughs weakly.

I know, failed in my patriotic duty. I know.

Laughs.

Look, Helmut, I'm after some advice. I've got Bishop von Galen coming to see me tonight. That's right, the one who's making all the fuss. And I wanted to check what line we're taking nowadays. In public, I mean.

Pause.

I see.

Longer pause.

Right.

Pause.

Right.

Pause.

But surely…?

Pause.

But what's the public line?

Pause.

For the common good. I see.

Pause.

A criminal waste of public money, I see.

Pause.

I thought I should emphasise our attempts to help the families – Yes, I remember her letter to the Führer.

Pause.

But what if he threatens to go public? I mean there a lot of Catholics around here, you know and I'm sure they'd listen.

Pause.

Right. And your office is happy to do that? Because I really don't think –

Pause.

I mean, I'm just a doctor, I don't know, I can't really –

Pause.

So you want me to tell him that?

Laughs nervously.

Well, if you say so.

MARTHA *enters and starts talking before she sees that* VICTOR *is on the phone.*

MARTHA. Doctor, Eric said that…

VICTOR. Martha, please… No, Helmut, here I am. It's just my maid just – Yes, where were we?

Pause.

I see.

Pause.

I see. 'Lives unworthy of – '

He looks nervously at MARTHA *who is waiting there.*

Right.

Pause. Laughing.

Yes, yes, Helmut, of course I'll be polite, who do you think I am?

Pause.

Yes, of course, and my regards to your wife.

Pause.

Of course, I remember her. She's –

Goodbye.

Pause.

Heil Hitler.

Puts the phone down.

MARTHA. I'm sorry I interrupted –

VICTOR. No, no, he's just an old friend. From medical school. Just a catch-up.

MARTHA. Nice.

VICTOR (*flat*). Yes.

Pause.

MARTHA. What's the matter?

VICTOR. Nothing, nothing.

Pause.

Feels like a lifetime ago, that's all.

MARTHA. How long ago was it?

VICTOR. I can't remember.

Pause.

When the world was young, I suppose.

Pause.

We were such idealists, in those days. Medicine, medicine, always medicine. For the good of all. Silly really.

Pause.

Sorry, I'm –

Pause.

So how can I help you?

MARTHA. Well, Herr Schmidt said you wanted to see me.

VICTOR. Yes, Martha, we have an important visitor this evening.

MARTHA. He told me.

VICTOR. And we need to make him welcome.

MARTHA. Well, of course, I'll make sure everything's –

Pause.

Why's he coming, do you think?

VICTOR. Well, he wants to talk – about the clinic, I think.

MARTHA. Support the work you're doing for the children?

VICTOR. No doubt.

MARTHA. And pray for them, I hope. The poor mites. I'm sure he'll pray for them.

Wells up. Crosses herself.

VICTOR. Yes.

MARTHA. He's such a holy man, you know, some people even say that he could be Pope one day, if they ever wanted a German Pope, which they probably won't! But he's a cardinal now, you know.

VICTOR. Of course, you're still a great believer, aren't you, Martha?

MARTHA. Well, I'm not Jewish, you know.

VICTOR. And you go to church?

MARTHA. Of course.

VICTOR. Well, good. I didn't think many people went to church nowadays, what with the new – ? I've never really understood the point of it all. But whatever makes you –

MARTHA. We go every Sunday. And feast days. I wouldn't
   stop that. Not for the world. And my children have been
   brought up in the Church. The two older ones don't go any
   more. But I take Friedrich every Sunday and we pray for his
   father's safe return.

VICTOR. Very good. Are you worried about that?

MARTHA. I don't know what to think.

VICTOR. It's hard, isn't it? Keeping the faith. In good things
   happening.

MARTHA. It is. It is.

   Pause.

   But you see, Doctor, whatever people say, the Pope's still in
   charge, of us Catholics at least. I know all about the Party, of
   course, and my Christof voted Nationalist way back in the
   twenties and though I'm not in the Party myself – I just
   never got round to it – I know that it's the best thing for
   Germany. It's just that I believe in the traditional way of
   doing things – call me old fashioned, if you like, but the
   Church is, well, you know, my home. Nothing wrong with
   that, is there? It's just family, not anything political or –

VICTOR. No, no, of course not, if that's what you believe in.
   We all need something to believe in, don't we?

MARTHA. Yes. And that's what I believe in.

VICTOR. Good. I'm glad.

   Pause.

MARTHA. Doctor, may I ask you a question?

VICTOR. Of course.

MARTHA. It's about Herr Schmidt.

VICTOR. Herr Schmidt?

MARTHA. Yes. He's very good at his job, I know. And
   everything's got much more organised since he started here,
   what, three months ago. But –

VICTOR. Well?

Pause.

MARTHA. Can I say something? Just between you and me?

VICTOR. Of course.

MARTHA. Well, it's this.

Pause.

I don't trust him.

VICTOR. Really?

MARTHA. Yes. I saw him sneak a young girl into his room the other night. From the village. Not much older than my Grete. He says he's broken off with her now. But I don't like things like that. I really don't.

VICTOR. He's a young man, you know.

MARTHA. And greedy. Do you see the way he eats and drinks?

VICTOR. Well, he doesn't smoke.

MARTHA. Do *you* trust him?

VICTOR. I don't think I've given the matter much thought.

Pause.

Why shouldn't I?

MARTHA. I thought maybe you'd understand.

VICTOR. Well, maybe I don't.

Pause.

To tell you the truth I don't really understand things like that. I'm sorry, I –

Changes the subject.

And now, Martha, if you don't mind, I must get on. Would you fetch a bottle of Moselle from the cellar, Bernkastel-Kues '34, it's a decent year, I think, and make sure it's nicely chilled, eh? I'm sure the Bishop will appreciate it. Here's the key.

MARTHA. Of course.

Pause.

I still think that –

VICTOR. Thank you, Martha,

She curtsies and goes out. He goes back to his desk. And she returns moments later.

MARTHA. Forgive me, Doctor, but Frau Pabst is waiting out here. Remember, I told you earlier? One of the mothers.

VICTOR (*sharply*). What? Oh yes, well, show her in, I suppose –

MARTHA (*leaving*). Thank you.

(*Off.*) This way, please, the doctor's very busy –

MARTHA *ushers* ELIZABETTA *in. A gaunt working-class woman in her forties, in factory clothes. Very nervous.*

ELIZABETTA. I'm sorry, Doctor, I won't take up much time. Heil Hitler, I should have said, I'm sorry, I've just got off my night shift, and I came straight here on the bus, you see, and I'm all a bit – And, sorry, I'm still in my work clothes. I should have –

VICTOR. Don't worry. Please. Do come in. Thank you, Martha.

MARTHA *hesitates, unsure whether to leave* ELIZABETTA *with* VICTOR.

Martha!

MARTHA *leaves.*

ELIZABETTA. So this is your office, your – ? Where you – ?

VICTOR. It is.

ELIZABETTA. Thank you for agreeing to see me. I know you're busy.

VICTOR. Not at all. How can I help?

ELIZABETTA. Well, I've brought you a present, Doctor, I hope you like stollen. I know it's not Christmas any more but I thought you might…

VICTOR. How very kind.

ELIZABETTA. And I've got a tin of Stefan's favourite biscuits here, just what I could afford, you know, could I leave them here on the table? Maybe your maid could take them down to him?

VICTOR. Of course. Of course. Now then, what can I do for you?

Pause.

ELIZABETTA. Well, I wanted to say that it's wonderful, everything you're doing for my son, Doctor, and I wanted to thank you. Stefan's been such a worry to me, over the years. He's a lovely boy, you know – well, a man now really – but he's never been able to speak properly, not at all in fact, and he's so thin, wafer thin, poor lad, he's not as clever as, well, most people, and I've had so many worries about him over the years, so it's good to know that he's here and that –

They both laugh embarrassed, for different reasons.

I was pleased as punch when he came here. It all got so hard for me at home and I know what people say, that things have changed for lads like him, but I don't believe them, I really don't. That's right, isn't it? He's safe here, isn't he?

VICTOR. Of course he is –

Pause.

ELIZABETTA. Good.

Pause.

D'you know, nobody knows what's wrong with him. I mean I'm sure *you* do, you're a doctor and everything, but nobody really knows. He went to loads of doctors in the old days, before, I mean. Someone said it must be my fault, you know, my mum and dad or something, it's in the blood, apparently, isn't it, it's the, er, what are they called?

VICTOR. Genes.

ELIZABETTA. That's right, genes. But there's nothing wrong with anyone in my family, thank God. We're all dead normal. My dad worked the Rhine, the barges, you know, and my old mum, she, well, bar work, mostly, you know, in Cologne –

VICTOR. I see.

ELIZABETTA. And then there's his shaking, you know, it's terrible sometimes, he just crashes to the ground, bangs his head, it's like this, look –

She shows it.

And sometimes it happens in public. And everybody just stares. People call him names: you know, 'epi', 'spazzy', things like that. A woman spat at him once. Said it was the devil trying to get out. That's cruel, don't you think? I don't believe in all that, it's just, erm –

VICTOR. Epilepsy.

ELIZABETTA. Yeah, epilepsy.

Pause.

Well, it got really bad five or six years ago, he was about seventeen, and the old doctor, well, he gave me some tablets which helped when he was little, but you can't get them any more, you know. Well, I'm sure *you* can, specialists and stuff, but not me from the pharmacy, and then he got so big, I couldn't pick him up when he fell over. I tried. But he's too heavy. And sometimes the shaking just goes on and on. I worry he'll swallow his tongue or fall down the stairs and break his head open or something. Or –

Pause.

You know. In the, erm – Drown.

Pause.

In the bath.

VICTOR. I see. And your husband?

ELIZABETTA. Long dead, may he rest in peace.

Crosses herself.

November 1917, you know, Battle of Cambrai, tanks. They never found his body, and I've brought Stefan up all by myself. Never met his dad. It's been hard.

VICTOR. I'm sure.

ELIZABETTA (*cheering up*). Can't complain though. Thank God for his big brother, Otto, is what I say.

VICTOR. Oh yes?

ELIZABETTA. Good lad. A really good lad.

VICTOR. A good family is important.

ELIZABETTA. It is.

Pause.

(*Holding back tears.*) It's important.

Pause.

I'd best be off. I've got, erm, things to do. I'm sorry to disturb you, I just wanted to, erm –

VICTOR. No, no, not at all. Any time.

ELIZABETTA. Thank you. Thank you very much. And happy new year, eh? 1941's going to be a good one, I think, don't you? That's what everyone says. Fingers crossed, eh? Fingers crossed.

Longish pause.

VICTOR. Well?

ELIZABETTA. I just wish I could see him. Just for a second. Give him a hug, you know. He's never been away from me, not even for a single night, and I miss him so much. It's been, what, nearly a year now. He's a funny boy, really. Lovely, I think, but I would say that, wouldn't I? Some people think that I must be ashamed of him, that he must be the worst thing that could have ever happened to me, that he must have ruined my life. And other people say, oh you're amazing, I don't know how you do it, but the truth is I just love him. That's all. I miss him.

Pause.

Couldn't I see him, just for a moment?

Pause.

Please.

VICTOR. It's the regulations, I'm afraid, Frau – ?

ELIZABETTA. Pabst. Frau Pabst.

Pause.

I understand. It's just that – Look I know he's different and that he ain't like most children, most young men I should say now, shouldn't I? He'd be a soldier by now, wouldn't he, if he'd turned out normal?

VICTOR. I suppose so. There are a lot of soldiers now –

ELIZABETTA. And he costs a load of money, doesn't he, people keep telling me that. So much money. And I know he's never going to get a job, even with all the jobs at the moment. Well, what could he do? He couldn't get work in a factory. They don't want him in the army, you know. You'd think they'd –

VICTOR. Frau Pabst, I really must –

ELIZABETTA. But some people have got so much money, haven't they, big houses and all that, I've seen them in Cologne from the tram, and the soldiers and the guns and, you know, everything, and I just think, well, I just think that's what the money's for, isn't it? Looking after people who –

VICTOR. Maybe.

Pause.

Maybe it is.

ELIZABETTA. I'm sorry, Doctor, but I've no one else to talk to and –

Pause.

Well, sometimes I just feel a bit lonely. That's all.

VICTOR. I do understand.

ELIZABETTA. And I don't really know what the point is. I come home from work – long shifts now, you know – and I heat up a bit of soup, some bread if I can get it, and I just sit there and look at his empty bed. Nothing else to do, is there? Just sit there and stare at his empty bed.

VICTOR. Frau Pabst, at least you have a job, not like –

ELIZABETTA. Yes, that's good, isn't it? I've got a job. Not everyone's –

Pause.

So, that's good.

Pause.

Doctor, can I ask you something?

VICTOR *gestures 'go ahead'.*

Do you have children, Doctor?

VICTOR. Sadly no.

ELIZABETTA. Then it's probably hard for you to understand. But it's this: I love Stefan just as much as I love his big brother. Funny, isn't it? Otto's in the Air Force, you know. A cook. My two beautiful boys. One all big and strong and – and the other, well, different. Just different.

Pause.

But what I want to know is what's going to happen to them? What with the war and everything. What do you – ? I mean if – ?

She starts to well up.

VICTOR. Please, Frau – ?

ELIZABETTA. I'm sorry. Yes, I'm going now. Goodbye. Thank you very much. I'm so sorry.

VICTOR. Not at all.

ELIZABETTA. It's just I sometimes worry that – that –

Starts to well up again.

Oh, it doesn't matter. Thank you. Goodbye.

VICTOR. Goodbye. And thank you for the cake.

She goes. He goes to the files. We hear him muttering to himself.

What was the name, again? Oh yes, P–A–B –

He sings the first phrase of 'Mackie Messer' to himself ('Und der Haifisch, der hat Zähne') without acknowledging the incongruity of it until he suddenly stops.

Ah there we are.

He carries the relevant box file over to his desk and starts to read Stefan's notes. Stops suddenly.

Oh, fuck.

He lights a cigarette. Coughs.

MARTHA *comes in with a tray of coffee.*

MARTHA. That's a nasty cough, Doctor, and it's getting worse. You really should stop smoking. I'm sorry to nag but it's true. Anyway, I've brought you some fresh coffee. I thought you might need it.

No reply.

Something wrong?

VICTOR. No, no, just that woman.

MARTHA. Us mothers, eh? We're all the same. Here, have some coffee.

VICTOR *(about the cake)*. She left that, as a gift.

MARTHA. How kind.

VICTOR. And there are some biscuits for her boy. Could you ask the nursing team to, to – ?

MARTHA. But they're not allowed food parcels any more. Remember?

VICTOR. Yes, well, I suppose you'd better have them then. Give them to your son: I'm sure he'd like them. And the cake, too, would you mind? I can't bear stollen.

MARTHA. Is that permitted? I mean, they weren't meant for me.

VICTOR. Of course it is.

MARTHA. Thank you. Friedrich will love them. I don't often get sweet – Are you sure it's all right?

No answer. Pause as MARTHA *wraps up the cake and Stefan's biscuits and is about to leave.*

VICTOR (*suddenly*). So, Martha, may I ask you a question.

MARTHA. Of course.

VICTOR. It's about your children. You don't mind, do you?

MARTHA. No, why should I?

VICTOR. Well, it's this. Do you ever worry about them?

MARTHA. Whatever do you mean?

VICTOR. Their health, their development.

MARTHA. They're all normal, you know.

VICTOR. Yes, yes, of course, it's just there are lots of different kinds of –

Pause.

Doesn't matter.

MARTHA. I worry about their future, if that's what you mean. The sooner this terrible war is over the better, if you ask me. But, actually, I think that isn't the most important thing.

VICTOR. What isn't?

MARTHA. Their health. And how well they do, at school and everything. I think it's morals that matter most. That's what the Führer says, isn't it, and I think he's right. We have to sacrifice ourselves for the good of all, don't we?

VICTOR. Of course.

MARTHA. And that's what matters. Morals come first.

VICTOR. And food later?

MARTHA. I beg your pardon?

VICTOR. Oh nothing.

MARTHA. I just think there are some things more important than being clever. Or being healthy. Or being successful, or rich. Or –

VICTOR. Such as?

MARTHA. Well, living a good life.

VICTOR. And do you live a good life?

MARTHA. I hope so. I think so.

VICTOR. And your children?

MARTHA. Well, Hans can be a bit boisterous. All that beer.

VICTOR. The military will sort that out, I'm sure.

MARTHA. I sometimes think they encourage it.

She laughs.

But it's Grete I really worry about.

VICTOR. Why's that?

MARTHA. Well, she's such a pretty girl, I know, but she knows it too. And that's what I worry about. Particularly with her father away.

VICTOR. I thought you said she was too young for all that?

MARTHA. She is. But it doesn't stop her. She says she's going to Cologne at the weekend. With one of her girlfriends. They're going to look at the cathedral and do some shopping, and go to a film, and stay in a youth hostel, she says. But she won't tell me who her friend is. I think she's hiding something from me.

VICTOR. What could she be hiding?

MARTHA. Well, Doctor, I think she's got a boyfriend there. I just hope she's careful. I don't want her saddled with a baby just yet, thank you very much.

VICTOR. No.

MARTHA. I know the Führer wants us to have lots of lovely babies, and he's right there, of course, but she's a bit young for that sort of thing, I think, don't you?

VICTOR. I'm sure you're imagining things.

MARTHA. I hope so. But she should wait until she can get married. I think it's disgusting, don't you agree?

VICTOR. Yes, well –

MARTHA. Marriage is for children. And children are for marriage. It's simple, isn't it?

VICTOR. I suppose so. I don't know.

MARTHA. Well I just worry, that's all.

VICTOR. I'm sorry to hear that. I wish I could help.

ERIC enters.

Ah, Herr Schmidt.

ERIC. Time for the ward round, Doctor.

VICTOR. Already?

ERIC. It's ten to –

VICTOR. Right.

ERIC (*turning to* MARTHA). Heil Hitler, Frau Trondheim.

MARTHA (*flustered*). Heil Hitler.

ERIC. Such a beautiful morning, isn't it, Frau Trondheim? Cold but bright. Makes you feel glad to be alive.

MARTHA. Here, let me help you, Doctor.

VICTOR takes off his jacket and she helps him put on his white coat. He looks like a real doctor now.

VICTOR. Thank you.

Pause.

So, Herr Schmidt, what do you think? Is Martha's daughter too young to have a boyfriend?

ERIC. I beg your pardon?

VICTOR. Well?

ERIC. How old is your daughter, Frau Trondheim?

MARTHA. Seventeen.

ERIC. Excellent.

VICTOR. Martha thinks she's too young.

ERIC. What's her name again?

MARTHA. Grete. I've told you.

ERIC. Ah, yes, Grete. Margrete. Good German name.

VICTOR. Well, what do you think?

ERIC. I think it's perfectly natural.

MARTHA. What do you mean?

ERIC. Well, a beautiful young woman – she is beautiful, isn't she, you showed me her picture –

MARTHA. You've not met her?

ERIC. I don't think so.

MARTHA. That's funny, I thought you had.

ERIC. How could I have?

MARTHA. I don't know.

Pause.

So what's natural about it?

ERIC. Well, a young woman like that, at the height of her –

MARTHA. Herr Schmidt, really.

ERIC. I'm just telling you the truth. It's a scientific fact.

VICTOR. All right, Eric, all right. That's enough of that.

MARTHA. You're a bad man, Eric Schmidt, a very bad man.

ERIC (*laughing*). And you, my dear Frau Martha Trondheim, are a perfect mother.

MARTHA. Doctor, I'm going home for a few hours now, if you don't mind. I need to make sure Friedrich's better, he's with my mother, you know, she helps out, but she's getting on a bit and keeps forgetting things. I'll be back in time for the Bishop. I've got to take the Christmas tree down today anyway. It's the Feast of the Epiphany.

Pause.

And as for you, Herr Schmidt, you should be ashamed of yourself. That's no way to talk.

ERIC. Frau Trondheim, I salute you. Heil Hitler.

MARTHA. Honestly. Heil Hitler.

She leaves. He laughs.

ERIC. What was that all about?

VICTOR. You tell me.

ERIC. And may I ask you, Doctor, was it you who put her up to this?

VICTOR. I beg your pardon.

ERIC. It was, wasn't it?

VICTOR. No, but it's you who's taking her daughter to Cologne, isn't it?

ERIC. And if it is?

VICTOR. What about her mother?

ERIC. What about her?

VICTOR. Can't you see?

ERIC. What?

VICTOR. The pain. The worry. Just look at her. Honestly.

ERIC. Oh please.

VICTOR. I just think that –

ERIC. Doctor, please, with great respect, this is a private matter and outwith your responsibility.

VICTOR. I thought we'd abolished private life?

ERIC. Ha, ha, Doctor, very funny.

Pause.

But perhaps not quite as funny as you thought.

VICTOR. Perhaps.

Pause.

So, all's calm on the wards?

ERIC. Mostly. A bit of a row last night on C, I gather. The nurses had to sedate one of the females.

VICTOR. But otherwise calm?

ERIC. Apparently.

VICTOR (*does up the buttons on his coat*). Good.

Pause.

Did you know that one of the mothers came to see me earlier?

ERIC. No.

VICTOR. Martha let her in. A Frau, oh damn it, what's he called, the –

ERIC....?

VICTOR. Pabst, that's it. – Well, we've got her son with us.

ERIC. Ah yes. Stefan Pabst. Stunted growth. Idiocy. Epilepsy. Obsessive type.

VICTOR. She wanted to see him.

ERIC. What did you say?

VICTOR. I told her she couldn't.

ERIC. Correct. And did you give any reasons?

VICTOR. I said it was against the regulations.

ERIC. Correct again.

Pause.

It would have been awkward if you'd allowed her to.

VICTOR (*smiles grimly*). Yes. The poor boy.

Pause.

And she gave me a stollen.

ERIC. Very generous.

VICTOR. I gave it to Martha. Disgusting stuff.

ERIC. You don't like Christmas, do you?

VICTOR. No.

ERIC. I love it.

VICTOR. Of course you do. Pure kitsch.

ERIC. Family. Friendship. I love it.

VICTOR. And the carols?

ERIC. Oh yes. Complete rubbish, of course, but – so beautiful.

Starts to sing 'Stille Nacht, Heilige Nacht' and stops himself.

VICTOR. Very good.

Pause.

And, you know, I looked at her, standing in my office, just there, and I found myself wondering what her life must be like.

ERIC. What?

VICTOR. Well, she lost her husband in the last war. Mashed by a tank, by the sound of it. And her older son is in the Luftwaffe, he's a cook, in some godforsaken place, and who knows if he'll ever come back.

ERIC *laughs*.

ERIC. He probably will. They need cooks. They're kept in the rear.

VICTOR. And now she works in a factory in Cologne. Night shift. Making artillery shells. 'Birthday presents for Winston.'

Pause.

And then there's her 'little Stefan'. Her idiot child. And she had to lose him too, didn't she. Not that she knows that yet, but – I mean, what a life. What a bloody awful life. Don't you think?

ERIC. Perhaps, but –

Pause.

Who knows.

Pause.

Who cares?

VICTOR. You really have no powers of empathy at all, do you? It's like you have –

Pause.

Anyway, I thought, just for a brief little moment –

Pause.

– that I hate this job.

Pause.

I mean, why the hell are we doing it?

Pause. Shrugs, almost laughing.

Stupid, isn't it?

ERIC. What on earth do you mean?

VICTOR. I mean that I don't know the answer to that question any more.

ERIC. I see. Well that's serious.

Pause.

Look, Doctor Franz, you're a good man. You became director of this clinic fifteen years ago, wasn't it, and you've worked miracles here. Looking after sick children. Helping them. And everyone admires you for it. Your long years of service, and so on. And now you're a senior consultant paediatrician, for Christ's sake. But this is more important, the work that you're doing now. For the country. For our new country. This is what really matters.

VICTOR. It's just –

ERIC. These youngsters here, they're nothing, really they aren't. It's not their fault they're like they are, I know, but what we do doesn't hurt them. In fact, most of them have no idea what's happening. No understanding at all. The Führer's right: they're leading 'lives unworthy of life'. It's as simple as that. 'Lives unworthy of life.'

Pause.

Come on. We've got work to do to.

Pause.

(*Sharp.*) Come on.

Pause.

VICTOR. Right.

They leave.

Schubert plays.

ACT TWO

Early evening of the same day. The room is dark and empty.
The curtains are open. Moonlight.

MARTHA *enters. She's evidently upset about something. She*
turns two sidelights on, draws the curtains, and lights the stove.
This should take the time it takes.

ERIC *enters suddenly.*

ERIC. Making everything nice and cosy for the Bishop?

MARTHA. I am.

ERIC. All spick and span for his holiness?

Grabs her from behind.

MARTHA (*sharply*). Herr Schmidt, please.

ERIC laughs.

VICTOR enters.

Doctor, can I talk to you for a moment?

VICTOR. If you wish.

MARTHA. In private, if you don't mind.

Pause.

Please.

VICTOR. Very well. Herr Schmidt, would you – ?

ERIC. Yes?

Pause. VICTOR looks at ERIC, silently ordering him out.

Doctor Franz.

VICTOR. Two minutes, Herr Schmidt.

ERIC. This is outrageous.

VICTOR. Thank you.

ERIC. We'll speak later. Heil Hitler.

ERIC leaves. MARTHA *closes the door behind him.*

VICTOR. Well?

MARTHA. It's him.

VICTOR. What is?

MARTHA. With Grete.

VICTOR. But that's –

Pause.

MARTHA. I don't know. They've been seeing each other for
   months apparently. She told me earlier, when I went home to
   give Friedrich his tea. I confronted her, I said, so who is it
   you're going to Cologne with, and she finally told me,
   straight out, I'm going to Cologne with Eric Schmidt, who
   works at the clinic. And when I said that it was all wrong,
   she said that I'm just an old woman, and I don't understand
   these things. So I said what about your father, and our priest,
   what would they say, and she just said that stuff didn't matter
   any more, it's a new world, didn't I realise, and anyway,
   she's in love with Herr Schmidt. Or so she said.

VICTOR. I see.

MARTHA. I hope you're being careful, I said, but apparently
   he wants a baby. For the Führer, apparently. I mean the
   Führer can have his own babies, can't he, but nowadays
   good German stock – I think it's disgusting, don't you, but
   what can I do about it? What can I do?

VICTOR. Are they going to get married?

MARTHA. I don't know. He doesn't like marriage. It's for
   'Catholic prudes', apparently.

VICTOR. I see. Well, he is from Lutheran stock, but –

MARTHA. Would you have a word with him?

VICTOR. Me? What can I say?

MARTHA. For my sake.

VICTOR. I don't know what to –

Pause.

MARTHA. Please.

VICTOR. I don't really understand such things, you know, no
children of my own, and so on –

Pause.

– but, yes, I'll have a word with him if you like.

Pause.

I suppose.

MARTHA. Thank you.

VICTOR. Was that it?

MARTHA. For now. Yes.

Pause.

VICTOR. Perhaps, you could just give me a drop –

MARTHA. All gone, I'm afraid. This morning, remember?

VICTOR. What a shame.

MARTHA. I'll come back later.

VICTOR *coughs again, badly.*

Oh, Doctor, I worry about you, I really do.

VICTOR. I'm fine, thank you.

MARTHA. I hope so. I'll ask Herr Schmidt to –

MARTHA *leaves.* VICTOR *left alone for a moment. Stares
into the stove. Moments later,* ERIC *comes in.*

ERIC. Well? What's this all about?

VICTOR. Martha's not best pleased with you.

ERIC. This is deeply insulting, Doctor, as I'm sure you understand. Of course, you're the Director of the Clinic, but to treat the Head of Administration like this in front of the domestic staff is outrageous. It really is.

VICTOR. She's very young, her daughter.

ERIC (*astonished, after a brief pause*). So?

VICTOR. What do you mean, 'so'?

ERIC. It's my life.

VICTOR. But you're not married.

ERIC. Oh please. She's an adult.

VICTOR. Just about.

ERIC. She's seventeen, for God's sake.

VICTOR. And, as far as I know, that's illegal.

ERIC. Oh please, Doctor, who's ever going to –

VICTOR. And Martha's terribly upset.

ERIC. She'll get over it. Mothers do.

VICTOR. And what if Grete gets pregnant?

ERIC. She won't.

VICTOR. And if she does?

ERIC. One more lovely Aryan, is what I'd say.

VICTOR. And you'll look after the child?

ERIC. Of course. Really, Doctor, what's got in to you?

VICTOR. Well, it's just –

ERIC. Healthy babies 'serve the national community'. Ask the Führer.

VICTOR. I see.

ERIC. Anyway, it's natural, isn't it? Isn't that what we believe in, Doctor?

VICTOR. I wish you'd stop using the word 'natural' to justify your perversion.

ERIC. My 'ideology', don't you mean?

VICTOR. What?

ERIC. Don't you believe in nature?

VICTOR. Of course, but –

ERIC. The survival of the fittest? Isn't that what this is all about?

VICTOR (*under his breath*). Who knows, but it doesn't justify you fucking the maid's daughter.

ERIC (*laughing*). Oh, Doctor, that's brilliant. Absolutely brilliant.

VICTOR. You can be so vulgar.

ERIC. It was you who used foul language.

VICTOR. The lowest common denominator, isn't it? Like all you fanatics.

Pause.

Brutal and cruel. You have no capacity for –

ERIC. You worry me sometimes, Doctor Franz.

VICTOR. Oh, please –

ERIC. And anyway, we must be strong, Doctor. Strong.

VICTOR. So they say.

ERIC. This is a sacred task. And we need people with dedication. Fanatics, as you call us.

VICTOR. Which is why you got sent here, I suppose. Taking this place over. Changing everything. I used to heal children here. I used to try to help them. Little girls with leukaemia. Boys with – I mean –

ERIC. Look, Doctor, it's simple. You either support National Socialism or you don't. And if you don't support it, you oppose it.

VICTOR. Simplistic nonsense. I'm a doctor.

ERIC. Maybe, but right now you're giving in to the irrational. What we are doing is for the good of all. You must know that.

VICTOR. I'm not questioning that.

ERIC. What are you questioning then?

Pause.

Eh?

VICTOR. I'm questioning your personal morality.

ERIC. I see.

Pause.

I hope that's all.

Pause.

Because I'm worried – . There are dozens of younger doctors who'd happily take your place, you know.

VICTOR. I'm sure.

ERIC. And you've been signing off on these patients for three months now. It's a bit late to change your mind.

Pause.

So, shall we put all this behind us?

Pause.

Well?

VICTOR. Very well.

ERIC. And are you prepared for the visit?

VICTOR. Sort of.

ERIC. Good.

VICTOR. I rang Berlin.

ERIC. And what did they advise?

VICTOR. Emphasise cost. Morally neutral.

ERIC. Well, yes: 60,000 Reichsmarks to keep one of these scroungers alive is, well – You could put a normal kid through five years of first-class schooling for the same amount. I've got the breakdown here.

He opens his case and puts a document on his desk.

Nobody can argue with that, can they? Not even you. Look.

VICTOR *looks at the paper.*

Though priests don't understand money, do they? They don't pay tax, do they, what do you think, do they pay tax?

VICTOR. I've no idea.

ERIC. They certainly don't work for a living. But what's he worried about, anyway? We're hardly the first. I mean, look at the Americans. And those English liberals change their tune pretty bloody quickly when it comes to cripples, I can tell you. They don't like them at all.

VICTOR. No.

Pause.

I'll stress kindness, I think.

ERIC. I beg your pardon?

VICTOR. That we're kind in what we do.

Pause.

The way we do it. That it's an act of kindness.

ERIC. Good.

VICTOR. And that it helps the families. I mean who'd want one of these as a child?

ERIC. Excellent.

Pause.

VICTOR. So are you going to stay away from Martha's daughter?

ERIC. Oh, Doctor Franz, really –

He's just leaving when a noise is heard in the hall.

MARTHA (*off*). You can't go in there, Frau Pabst, he's in a meeting.

ELIZABETTA (*off*). I have to see him.

Both women burst in.

MARTHA. Doctor, I'm so sorry, she wouldn't take no for an answer. I said you were –

ERIC (*squaring up to* ELIZABETTA). What seems to be the problem, madam? How can I help?

ELIZABETTA. I want to talk to the doctor.

ERIC. He's busy, I'm afraid. Talk to me, I work with him.

ELIZABETTA. No, I want to talk to the doctor.

ERIC. I'll get the guard.

Goes towards the door.

VICTOR. No, no, let her talk. I'll deal with it.

ERIC. I beg your pardon?

VICTOR. Yes, just leave us alone.

Pause.

Please. Leave us alone.

ERIC (*under his breath*). Bloody hell.

Leaves.

MARTHA. You can't just barge in like this, Frau Pabst. Doctor Franz, I told her, I said –

VICTOR. It's all right, Martha. Leave us, would you?

MARTHA. Are you sure? The Bishop will be here soon you know and –

VICTOR. Yes, yes, Martha, I know, thank you.

MARTHA. Well I'll be next door if you need me.

Pause.

What should I do if he – ?

VICTOR. Just show him in.

She leaves.

Now then, Frau –

ELIZABETTA. Pabst. P–A–B–S–T.

VICTOR. Ah, yes, Frau Pabst. How nice to see you again.

ELIZABETTA. It's toasty in here, isn't it? Lovely and –

VICTOR. What is it you wanted to see me about?

ELIZABETTA. It's so cold tonight.

VICTOR. I've not been out.

ELIZABETTA. I got your letter, you see. When I got home today. After I'd been here… And I've come straight back here, no sleep.

VICTOR (*vaguely*). Letter?

ELIZABETTA. From the clinic. About Stefan. Remember?

Pause.

VICTOR. I see.

ELIZABETTA. It's got your signature on it.

Shows him the letter.

There, that's you, isn't it?

VICTOR. It is.

Pause.

ELIZABETTA. So, you must have known.

VICTOR. What?

ELIZABETTA. This morning, when I came to see you, you must have known. Look at the date. That's three days ago, isn't it? You must have known.

VICTOR. Known what?

ELIZABETTA. What happened.

VICTOR. Not really.

ELIZABETTA. But you're the doctor. You look after people, don't you? Isn't that your job?

VICTOR. It's a big clinic, you know. A lot of people –

ELIZABETTA. Yes, but I told you my name.

VICTOR. I'm not good at names.

ELIZABETTA. And I told you about my son.

VICTOR. Yes. Hardly any speech. Severely retarded. Epilepsy. Is that right?

ELIZABETTA. No speech, Doctor. Not a word.

Pause.

And this letter says that he's dead. I'll read it to you, shall I?

Pause.

'Dear Frau Pabst,

We regret to inform you that your son, Stefan Karlheinz Pabst, died of natural causes at 8.32 p.m. on December 29th 1940.

Yours sincerely, Doctor Victor Franz, Director and Senior Paediatric Consultant, Winkelheim Clinic.'

Pause.

That's what it says, doesn't it? I'm not so good at reading, I'm afraid. Go on, you read it. Is that what it says?

Pause.

And that's your signature, isn't it?

VICTOR. It is.

ELIZABETTA. I thought so.

Pause.

So how did it happen? You're a doctor, aren't you? Tell me the truth.

VICTOR. I don't exactly know. Now, Frau Pabst, I've got a very important –

ELIZABETTA. You don't know how he died?

VICTOR. No, I don't.

Pause.

'Natural causes', it says here.

Pause.

Let me look it up. Excuse me.

He goes to the files and takes down the relevant box folder.

Ah yes, 'status epilepticus'. Blocked windpipe. Emergency procedures ineffective. I'm so sorry.

ELIZABETTA. So he didn't drown?

VICTOR. I beg your pardon?

ELIZABETTA. In the bath?

VICTOR. No. That's not what it says here.

ELIZABETTA. Thank God.

VICTOR. Why that, particularly?

ELIZABETTA. He nearly drowned when he was a lad. Must have been about seven. I was in the kitchen cooking Otto's tea and I'd put Stefan in the bath. I came in and his head was underwater. For just a few seconds, thank God, but it's my worst nightmare.

VICTOR. Well, he didn't drown.

ELIZABETTA. So how did he die then?

VICTOR. Blocked windpipe. As I said.

ELIZABETTA. Is that right?

Pause.

So when can I have the body?

VICTOR. I'm sorry, Frau Pabst –

ELIZABETTA. Why not?

VICTOR. Because –

Pause.

Well –

ELIZABETTA. Because what?

VICTOR. Because it's –

ELIZABETTA. Where is it?

Pause.

You've burnt it, haven't you?

VICTOR. Standard practice nowadays, I'm afraid. Clinical cremation.

ELIZABETTA. I see.

VICTOR. My condolences, Frau Pabst.

ELIZABETTA. Can I sit down for a sec?

VICTOR. Of course.

ELIZABETTA. I'm so tired all of a sudden.

Long pause.

Did you ever meet him?

VICTOR. Well, I must have done on my rounds.

ELIZABETTA. Let me show you something –

She takes out a picture.

VICTOR. Please, Frau Pabst.

ELIZABETTA. Beautiful, isn't he? His hair's so blond, it's almost white. 'A brilliant shock of brilliant blond hair.' That's what a friend of mine said.

VICTOR. Very handsome. Good Aryan stock.

ELIZABETTA. And such a lovely smile.

Pause.

And now – ?

VICTOR. Frau Pabst, please, I really must get on –

ELIZABETTA. Ashes?

Pause.

A little pot of ashes?

Pause.

Can I take them home with me? Put them on the mantelpiece? Dip my fingers in them?

VICTOR. Oh, please.

ELIZABETTA. Can I? They're my son's ashes.

VICTOR. In due course. They'll be sent to you.

ELIZABETTA (*dries her eyes*). Good. Thank you.

Pause.

VICTOR. Along with his effects.

Pause.

And the cremation costs, of course.

ELIZABETTA. I can't –

Pause.

Doctor, can I ask you a question?

VICTOR. If you like. But quickly, please –

ELIZABETTA. What's going to happen to Otto?

VICTOR. I beg your pardon?

ELIZABETTA. My eldest. He's in the Air Force. I told you. He's a cook. Is he going to have to die too?

VICTOR. Oh, I'm sure he'll be fine. They don't –

ELIZABETTA. Because I'm all alone, you know. My old man's dead. At least I've got a job. But without Otto I'd be finished. Finished.

Pause.

D'you understand?

VICTOR. Please, Frau Pabst.

ELIZABETTA. You see, I thought you were going to look after Stefan. I thought that's why he was here. What this place was for. Looking after people who –

VICTOR. Now, now, Frau Pabst.

ELIZABETTA. That's what you were meant to do, isn't it?
Look after people who can't look after themselves. Isn't that
why we work so blinking hard, pay all that tax –

Pause.

I thought you were going to look after him, not let him
drown.

Pause.

Well, you didn't let him drown, but you know what I mean.
You –

Pause. Tears welling.

I'm sorry, I shouldn't, crying is weak, I know, and we're not
meant to cry, we're meant to be brave and all that, lay down
our lives for the country, but I'm just a woman, you know,
a mother, and –

Pause.

I just feel –

Pause.

I feel –

VICTOR. Please, Frau –

ELIZABETTA. I mean, you should've seen them when they
were small, they played so nicely together. Well, Otto played
with Stefan. Stefan wasn't much good at playing with
anyone. But Otto always kept an eye out for him, if anyone
bullied him for being different, you know, a spastic or
whatever, he'd beat them up, beat the crap out of them. And
now I've lost Stefan and God knows if I'll ever see Otto
again. What can I do, eh? What am I going to do?

VICTOR. It's hard.

ELIZABETTA. And I'm getting old. I'm forty-five. I'm past it.
Nearly.

Pause.

But there's something I need to ask you.

Pause.

And I want you to tell me the truth.

VICTOR. Of course.

ELIZABETTA. It's this.

Pause.

I know that my Stefan is, well, *was* different. Very different.
There were all sorts of things he couldn't do. He couldn't do
hardly anything, in fact. He was pretty bloody useless.

Pause.

But it wasn't the epilepsy that killed him, was it? It was
something else, wasn't it? I'm right, aren't I?

Pause.

Aren't I?

Pause.

I'm not stupid, you know. I'm not like Stefan. I know I just
work in a factory, making artillery shells for the front,
earning rubbish money, I know I'm just another bloody war
widow, with one daft son and another who's a cook, but
something's going on here, isn't it. The rumours are right,
aren't they? This is – it's – ? Like one of them camps, isn't
it? KZ, isn't it?

VICTOR *is silent.*

This isn't a clinic, is it? You're not a doctor, are you? Even
with all them certificates. You're a –

Pause.

This –

Pause.

This stinks. That's what it does. It stinks.

VICTOR. Really, Frau Pabst –

ELIZABETTA. The whole lot of it. You think you're so clever, don't you, you think what you're doing is good for everyone, for 'Grossdeutschland' as you call it –

Pause.

But it's not good for my poor Stefan, is it? I thought it was, but I was wrong – but let me tell you something, Doctor. We're going to have to pay for all this, you know that, don't you? All of us. I had a dream last night: Cologne, where I come from, my home, completely flattened. The whole city. Miles and miles of ruins. Bridges, houses, the lot. Just the spires of the cathedral still standing.

Pause. Gestures.

Two fingers pointing up to heaven. Fuck you, God.

Pause.

It's true.

Pause.

So why did you kill him then?

VICTOR. What?

ELIZABETTA. Why did you kill him?

VICTOR. I didn't kill him.

ELIZABETTA. So who did?

VICTOR. I don't know. But it wasn't me.

Pause.

I'm a doctor. I cure people.

ELIZABETTA. Do you? Really?

Pause.

I don't know who to believe any more. Politicians, doctors, judges. They're all as bad as each other. This country's – completely –

VICTOR. Now, Frau Pabst, that's no way to –

ELIZABETTA. But he *was* killed, wasn't he? Someone killed him, didn't they?

Pause.

Didn't they?

Pause.

Didn't they?

VICTOR (*finally*). Yes.

ELIZABETTA. Why was that?

VICTOR. Because –

Pause.

He was killed because of his condition. Because he'll never be able to make a contribution to society. Because looking after him costs too much money – and because –

Pause.

ELIZABETTA. Yes?

VICTOR. Because there's no need for such people in the Third Reich.

ELIZABETTA. No need?

VICTOR. That's right.

Pause.

He felt no pain. His life of suffering is finally over. You should be relieved.

Pause.

ELIZABETTA. Do you have children, Doctor?

VICTOR. No.

ELIZABETTA (*approaches* VICTOR). Oh yeah, you told me.

Pause.

So, you have no idea what this feels like, do you?

VICTOR. No, I suppose I don't. I suppose I have no –

She stares at him and there is no answer. Suddenly she spits in his face.

VICTOR *is visibly shocked for a second but controls himself, wipes his face with a handkerchief and calmly goes to the door and calls.*

Martha, could you come in here a moment?

MARTHA *appears. There is a struggle and the following should overlap.*

MARTHA. Doctor?

VICTOR. Would you show Frau Pabst the way out?

ELIZABETTA. You keep your hands off me –

VICTOR. Frau Pabst is very upset. Her son died –

ELIZABETTA. No, you said he'd been –

VICTOR. Martha, please, can you show her the way out?

MARTHA. Come on, Frau Pabst. I'm sure it's for the best –

ELIZABETTA. What do you know about it – ?

MARTHA. Come on, I'm sure there's been a misunderstanding.

ELIZABETTA *refusing to be cosseted, gestures violently at* VICTOR, *and leaves shouting with* MARTHA *protesting and urging her to 'come along'.*

ELIZABETTA. Fuck you, Doctor. Fuck you. Fuck you.

There is a pause. VICTOR *checks his watch. Coughs. Gathers his thoughts. Stokes the stove. Lights candles on the stove and on the table. It grows quiet and still. Eventually, a car draws up outside.* VICTOR *pulls the curtain aside and glances out of the window. A doorbell rings in the distance. Voices off.*

MARTHA *comes back in with* BISHOP GALEN *and announces him.*

MARTHA. His reverence, Bishop von Galen.

VICTOR. Thank you, Martha.

MARTHA. Will that be all, Doctor?

VICTOR. Yes, could you bring in the wine?

MARTHA (*about to leave*). Doctor, excuse me, but –

VICTOR. Martha. The wine. Immediately.

As she turns to leave.

Thank you.

Turning, finally, to GALEN.

Good evening, your reverence, and welcome to Winkelheim.

GALEN. Thank you, Doctor. And for agreeing to meet me.

(*About* MARTHA.) Did you need to – ?

VICTOR. No, no. Nothing to worry about. Do please sit down. Here by the stove. It's a cold night.

GALEN. Thank you.

He sits.

VICTOR. Did you have a good drive?

GALEN. Icy, but my driver seemed to manage. And the countryside around here is –

VICTOR. Isn't it? Do you know the district?

GALEN. Not well. Bleak but beautiful. A winter's journey, one might almost say.

VICTOR. Indeed. And how are you finding Münster, your reverence?

GALEN. Big city, you know.

VICTOR. Well, you must be used to that from Berlin.

GALEN. Certainly.

VICTOR. And you know the new Pope from those days too, I gather.

GALEN. I do. A remarkable man.

MARTHA *comes on with the wine.*

VICTOR. So, your reverence, can I tempt you with a glass?

GALEN. Just some water, please.

VICTOR. Very well. Martha.

She leaves to get the water.

GALEN. But don't let me stop you.

VICTOR. No, no. One should never drink alone.

Pause. Eventually MARTHA *returns with a carafe of water and two glasses.*

GALEN (*to* MARTHA). Thank you.

MARTHA (*curtsies as she leaves*). Your reverence.

Pause.

GALEN. So, I'm sure you know why I've come.

VICTOR. Well, I'd heard –

GALEN. It's very simple.

VICTOR. Is it?

GALEN. Extremely. How should I begin? Well, let me put it as directly as I can: 'The right to life, to inviolability, and to freedom is an indispensable part of any moral social order.'

Pause.

What else needs to be said?

VICTOR. Yes, I read your letter.

GALEN. Well?

VICTOR. It's very carefully argued.

GALEN. And what is your response to its substance?

VICTOR. I think it's complicated.

GALEN. How so?

VICTOR. Because it is.

GALEN. It isn't. It's simple.

VICTOR. We seem to be simply exchanging assertions.

Pause.

Your reverence, may I ask you a question?

GALEN. If you must.

VICTOR. I hope you will forgive the bluntness, but –

Pause.

– do you love your country?

GALEN. Good Lord.

VICTOR. Do you see yourself as a patriot?

GALEN. I fail to –

VICTOR. Do you support the new Germany?

GALEN. I think the Versailles Treaty was an outrage, and the Weimar Republic even worse. So, thus far, yes.

VICTOR. And do you care about the poor?

GALEN. Doctor Franz, I fail to see where this is taking us, and I'd ask you to –

VICTOR. It's important.

Pause.

Well?

GALEN. I follow in Christ's footsteps, Doctor.

VICTOR. Despite your background?

GALEN. How dare you?

Stands.

VICTOR. Clemens August Graf von Galen. One of the oldest families in Germany.

GALEN. I'm proud of my forefathers.

VICTOR. I admire you for that. And for your commitment to the poor.

GALEN. I don't do it for your admiration.

Pause.

I do it because it's right.

VICTOR. I'm glad.

GALEN. I didn't come here to be insulted, Doctor Franz. Please ask your maid to show me the way down. Goodnight.

Makes to leave.

VICTOR. Forgive me, your reverence. Just a moment.

GALEN. Well?

VICTOR. With your permission, I'd like to tell you some uncomfortable truths. Which may answer some of your objections.

GALEN. I beg your pardon?

VICTOR. May I?

Pause.

Please. It may be useful.

GALEN. Doctor, do you have any idea who I am?

VICTOR. I do, and I'd like to talk to you. On a rational basis. Man to man.

Pause.

That's why you came, isn't it? To talk?

GALEN. It is.

Pause.

Very well. But be brief.

VICTOR. Thank you.

They both sit down again.

Your reverence, d'you know how much it costs to look after one of our young people for a year? A paraplegic cripple, for example.

GALEN. I don't.

VICTOR. Or a severely retarded child?

GALEN. Of course not. Why are you asking me?

VICTOR. Or a young man who is wheelchair-bound? Or all the other deeply troubling people we have in this clinic?

GALEN. Many of our honoured veterans are wheelchair-bound, Doctor.

VICTOR. That's different. They have intellectual capacity.

GALEN. Not all of them.

VICTOR. And we have issues with them too. And the insane or psychologically incompetent. But here are the figures, your reverence. Just look at them. They speak for themselves.

He hands GALEN *the sheet* ERIC *gave him earlier. Pause as* GALEN *looks at the figures.*

Do you know what that could buy? For the poor of Berlin. Or Hamburg. Schools, hospitals, roads. Food, even.

GALEN. And weapons.

VICTOR. Weapons too, certainly.

Pause.

But don't you see? These people cost the state a huge amount of money, an astonishing amount of money.

Pause.

And these are difficult times, your reverence, hard times, and so what we're doing here is for the good of all. Really it is.

GALEN. And the National Socialist state is going to use this money to help the poor, is it?

VICTOR. That's a decision for the government, not me.

Pause.

But I do know that if it wasn't for the Führer they'd be turning to the Church's old friend Karl Marx.

GALEN. Doctor Franz, I'm no socialist, as well you know. And never have been. I detest socialism.

VICTOR. National Socialism, then? You support that, don't you?

Pause.

Well?

Pause.

GALEN. I used to. I welcomed them in 1933.

VICTOR. Yes, Storm Troopers carried swastikas at your consecration. I remember the pictures. Bormann was delighted. 'One of us', he said.

GALEN. Well?

VICTOR. Well, where do you stand today?

GALEN. I'm a man of God. I give unto Caesar what is Caesar's.

VICTOR. And God what is God's. Yes, I know that one too.

GALEN. Franz – Doctor Franz – you're an intelligent man, I can tell. So let me tell you what I see. I see a government that has no respect for traditional values. A regime prepared to tear up centuries of tradition for its own corrupt purposes. Everywhere I look I see greed and immorality.

Pause.

Do you know why Hitler attacks the Church? Because he can't bear our moral authority. And because he wants our property. Your friends in the Gestapo have turned one of the Rhineland's most beautiful nunneries into an army brothel. Priests are thrown into concentration camps if they say anything controversial. Catholics are mocked in the newspapers and on the radio.

VICTOR. And what about the Jews?

GALEN. The Jews?

Pause.

That's completely different.

VICTOR. Is it?

GALEN. Before this war began, the Holy Father clearly condemned the exaltation of one race over another.

VICTOR. But now it's a matter of personal conscience, am I right?

GALEN. The Vatican has other things to worry about.

VICTOR. You've personally protested about the Jews too, I gather.

GALEN. Of course. It's one thing to say that they aren't real Germans, you could even say that they have no place in our Christian country. But what does Hitler plan to do, kill them all off, the ones who stay? It's unthinkable, this level of persecution.

VICTOR. Perhaps.

GALEN. And anyway, where would we be without the Jews? I mean, look at the Old Testament, what do they think that is? And as for this mystical nonsense that Rosenberg has come up with. Well it's quite preposterous.

VICTOR. You have no fear in speaking your mind, do you?

GALEN. I say what I know to be right.

VICTOR. But you must be aware of the possible consequences –

GALEN. Look, Doctor, I'm sixty-three. My health is, well, I've got maybe five more years. I must bear witness to the truth of the Gospels. That's all I can do.

VICTOR. Commendable.

GALEN. I'm glad you think so.

Pause.

Do you mind if I smoke a pipe?

VICTOR. I'll join you, if I may.

GALEN *lights up*. VICTOR *lights a cigarette*.

GALEN (*smiling*). My secret vice.

Pause.

So, this clinic of yours. Tell me about it. How does it operate?

VICTOR. Well, the Winkelheim Clinic is a centre, really, for all sorts of young people. Up to the age of twenty-five.

GALEN. And you founded it?

VICTOR. Fifteen years ago, in 1926. There was a Catholic home for crippled children here but it was closed as a result of, well, clerical improprieties, I'm afraid.

GALEN. I see. And this clinic is run for the benefit of – ?

VICTOR. All sorts, as I say.

GALEN. Moral degenerates?

VICTOR. A few, yes. Criminals, child prostitutes, and so on.

GALEN. And the others?

VICTOR. Spastics, cripples, retards. Incurables, you know.

GALEN. I see. Very difficult.

Pause.

And what happens to them here?

VICTOR. Well, we house them.

GALEN. Under guard?

VICTOR. Naturally.

GALEN. And you treat them?

VICTOR. Where we can make a difference.

GALEN. And do you make a difference?

VICTOR. Not as much as we used to. Budgetary constraints, you know. And these young people have very severe problems.

GALEN. But you try?

VICTOR. We do. We're pioneering some new treatments too.

GALEN. And you feed them, I presume?

VICTOR. Of course. Nothing excessive, but yes. And give them shelter.

GALEN. All of them?

VICTOR. Certainly.

GALEN. So these tales of starvation and frostbite are mere rumours?

Pause.

VICTOR. Of course.

Pause.

GALEN. But that's no longer relevant, is it?

VICTOR. Not entirely, no.

GALEN. Well?

VICTOR. What have you heard?

GALEN. We've been told that patients are being sent from here to their deaths.

VICTOR. There have always been deaths in clinics like these. Faulty procedures, accidents, natural causes. Epilepsy, mostly.

GALEN. 'Death by indifference'?

Pause.

VICTOR. Sometimes.

GALEN. But this is different, isn't it?

VICTOR. Only slightly.

GALEN....?

VICTOR. Well, as you obviously know, because you wouldn't ask me otherwise, since last autumn, the first Tuesday of every month, two grey coaches – with painted-out windows – come and take the most severely handicapped off to the Hadamar Institute.

GALEN. Near Limburg?

VICTOR. Correct.

GALEN. Where they're killed?

Pause.

VICTOR. Apparently.

Pause.

Mercy killings, your reverence.

GALEN. I see. They're gassed, I believe. Is that correct?

VICTOR. Perhaps. I've not been there myself.

GALEN. They are. We know for certain.

Pause.

And more than fifty thousand have been killed so far. Is that correct?

VICTOR. Not from here.

GALEN. But across the country?

VICTOR. Perhaps.

GALEN. 'Perhaps'? Is that all you can say? 'Perhaps'?

VICTOR. Your reverence, I don't know how many adults have been dealt with in this way, which is why I used the word 'perhaps'. All I know is what we do here. I believe in numbers and facts, not wild emotions. I'm a scientist.

GALEN. But you don't know how many adults have been murdered.

VICTOR. No. I only deal with children.

GALEN. I see.

Pause.

So how many children have been murdered?

VICTOR. I'm not sure. This has only been happening here since September last year.

Pause.

My administrator keeps the records.

GALEN. I see.

Pause.

And what is your opinion on all this? It's hardly why you
became a doctor, is it? A much-respected paediatrician?

VICTOR. No.

Pause.

But –

GALEN. Well?

VICTOR. Yes?

GALEN. What do you think about what's happening? Tell me.

VICTOR. Your reverence –

GALEN. What's your opinion? As a human being, I mean.

VICTOR. I think –

Long pause.

Well, it's terribly difficult.

Pause.

There you are.

GALEN. What on earth do you mean? 'It's terribly difficult,
there you are'?

Pause.

What does that mean?

VICTOR. It means –

Pause.

Exactly what it sounds like.

GALEN (*stands*). Let me tell you what I think, Doctor Franz.
I think this isn't a clinic, I think it's a charnel house. This is
the Massacre of the Holy Innocents, nothing less.

VICTOR. No, it isn't.

GALEN. How can you live with such a thing on your
conscience?

VICTOR. Bishop, you might have gathered that I'm not
a Christian.

GALEN. But you have a conscience, don't you? Or is that gone too, in this new world of yours?

VICTOR. If I were you I'd be a little more –

GALEN (*ignoring him*). This has nothing to do with being a Christian. It's about being a human being. We owe a duty of care to those who are weaker than us. We're not barbarians. This is Germany: the land of Goethe and Schiller. The *Matthew Passion*. How can we be doing this to our fellow human beings? It can't be true.

Pause.

VICTOR (*coughing*). Excuse me a moment.

He goes to the door and calls.

Martha. Martha, I think I'll have a glass of that wine after all.

There's a pause as MARTHA *brings the wine back and ceremoniously uncorks it and pours it.*

Your reverence?

GALEN. Just half a glass, thank you.

VICTOR. Thank you, Martha.

MARTHA. You're welcome, Doctor. Your reverence.

Curtsies and leaves.

VICTOR. Your health.

They toast.

GALEN. Mm. Excellent wine.

VICTOR. Look at the label.

GALEN. Ha! My cousin's vineyard. They own that side of the river. Right down to the bend. I used to go there as a child.

Laughs bitterly.

When the world was young.

Pause.

And what about you, Doctor, where were you brought up?

VICTOR. Dortmund. Nothing special.

GALEN. And medical school?

VICTOR. Munich.

GALEN. In the twenties?

VICTOR. I suppose so.

GALEN. Did you enjoy it?

VICTOR. I loved it.

GALEN. So why did you decide to study medicine?

VICTOR. Because – well, I wanted to help people, you know. And I found it intellectually stimulating.

GALEN. Paediatrics?

VICTOR. Yes. The next generation, you know.

GALEN. An idealist, then?

VICTOR. Perhaps. When the world was young.

GALEN. A party member now, I take it?

VICTOR. Had to be.

GALEN. And your staff?

VICTOR. Some of them. The administrative team, certainly.

GALEN. I see.

VICTOR. Young Schmidt is. The Chief Administrator. Very dedicated. SS, in fact. Dresses like a doctor though, for obvious reasons.

Pause.

Very effective.

GALEN. So, what do you plan to do now?

VICTOR. What do you mean?

GALEN. About what's happening here?

VICTOR. Bishop, it's not up to me. It's part of a much bigger programme.

GALEN. I know. But this clinic is the centre in the district. You can't avoid responsibility for that. We've been following the death notices. They're hardly standard, are they?

VICTOR. Our patients have very grave problems, you know. We do what we can to help them.

GALEN. But when you fail –

VICTOR. When it becomes hopeless we very gently and kindly turn off the tap. It hurts nobody. It's the best thing for everybody. I –

GALEN. Is that how you see it?

VICTOR. And, as I say, it saves a huge amount of money.

GALEN. Ah, money, money always, money. The measure of all things.

VICTOR. Your reverence, I'm sure you know a great deal about theology and, as a bishop, no doubt, you have some experience of money, perhaps even a great deal, but, with the greatest respect, I suspect you know nothing about medicine.

GALEN. Possibly.

VICTOR. So let me tell you. And it's difficult, this. But we have up to one hundred and twenty patients here at any one time. Many of them have only the simplest understanding of what is going on around them. Some have the intellectual functioning of the average one-year-old. At least three quarters have no speech, and the more capable just gibber incomprehensibly. Over half are confined to wheelchairs, with no control over their limbs. Many are incontinent at night, some in the daytime too. Epilepsy is common, from the mildest seizures to fully blown grands mals. Their life expectancy is limited and many won't see their thirtieth birthday.

GALEN. I see.

VICTOR. The vast majority are sexually immature and will never be able to become parents. A handful can hold down the simplest of jobs – they help in the kitchen and do other menial tasks – but most are incapable of the lowest forms of employment. They can never make a contribution to society, they pay no tax, and will never be able to give back even a fraction of what we provide them. They are, quite simply, the lowest of the low. It's hard to know how the German state – particularly in a time of war – can justify the expenditure, the professionalism required to keep them alive. It's as simple as that, your reverence. It's difficult but it's also simple.

GALEN. I see. So how do you make your choices? Of which ones to kill?

VICTOR. On simple medical criteria. We assess their cognitive abilities.

GALEN. And categorise them accordingly?

VICTOR. Exactly. Medical judgements have to be made.

GALEN. And the most severe go first? The weakest?

VICTOR. They do.

GALEN. And how will you know when to stop? Is there a limit?

VICTOR. Oh, your reverence, there are tens of thousands of such people, scattered across Germany and the occupied territories.

GALEN. And you intend to kill them all?

VICTOR. I'm just a doctor, your reverence, I don't have a –

GALEN. And these people that you kill are of all kinds, all ages?

VICTOR. In this clinic we only take people up to the age of twenty-five.

GALEN. And you're killing the youngest first, I gather?

VICTOR. Sometimes.

GALEN. Children as young as five, I'm told?

VICTOR. If necessary. Even younger.

GALEN. I see.

Pause.

VICTOR. We do it with kindness, your reverence. We are doctors, and we act like doctors.

GALEN (*sarcastically*). And what about the – ?

VICTOR. Hippocratic Oath? It's a great ideal. And it's guided me in my career, wherever possible. But we live in nuanced times, you know. We have limited means. We give one person the gift of life, and withhold it from another. All medicine is a matter of choices, of priorities, you know. People imagine there are absolutes, but doctors are always involved in making tough choices – between life and death, in fact. You must understand that.

GALEN. Moral relativism.

VICTOR. If you like.

Pause.

The facts of life, I prefer.

GALEN. I see.

Pause.

But let me ask you this, Doctor. Have you never come across the concept of the *sancta simplicita*?

VICTOR. No.

GALEN. And do you know why Christ died on the cross?

VICTOR. I'm afraid I don't believe in God. And my theology is –

GALEN. But you must believe in stories.

VICTOR. I have limited interest in fairytales, I'm afraid, your reverence.

GALEN. Christ died on the cross in agony. Nails through his hands and feet. A crown of thorns round his head. And was made to drink vinegar by sadistic guards. Familiar nowadays, really.

VICTOR. Yes.

GALEN. Nazis, that's right. And He died an innocent, the purest man who ever lived. He was the Lamb of God, and the embodiment of innocent human suffering. But in his suffering he saved us all. Do you understand what that means?

VICTOR. You think that the young people in my clinic are Christlike?

GALEN. I do. More than you or I or any of us. In their suffering, they can help us be better people.

VICTOR. Please, your reverence, try to understand, I don't believe in God. And I'm not interested in metaphors. They are who they are. Young people with –

GALEN. But you have your own gods, don't you?

VICTOR. Your reverence, I'm a scientist. I'm a doctor, it's as simple as that.

Pause.

Would you care for another glass of wine?

GALEN. Thank you.

VICTOR (*pours another glass*). And some cheese?

GALEN. Just a little.

VICTOR (*goes to the hall*). Martha. Martha.

She appears.

A nice plate of bread and cheese I think, don't you?

MARTHA (*smiling*). Of course.

Leaves.

GALEN. Thank you.

VICTOR. At least there's wine.

VICTOR *coughs badly.*

MARTHA (*comes in with the cheese*). Here you are, sir. Your reverence.

GALEN. Bread and wine. How biblical.

VICTOR. This is my maid. Frau Trondheim. She's a good Catholic, she says.

MARTHA (*curtsies*). Oh, your reverence, I'm such an admirer of yours. The way you stood up against the wickedness in the bad old days. All that carry-on in Berlin, and here in Cologne. You're an example to us all.

GALEN. Thank you, my child.

MARTHA. Would you –

Pause.

May I beg you for a –

GALEN. A blessing?

MARTHA. Would you mind?

GALEN. Of course. Who for, in particular?

MARTHA. Well, my children, if you don't mind.

Pause.

All our children.

She kneels and he says some Latin under his breath and blesses her.

Amen. Thank you, your reverence. Thank you.

VICTOR. Happy, Martha?

MARTHA. The ways of God are –

VICTOR (*to* GALEN). Mysterious?

GALEN. Exactly.

VICTOR. That'll be all, Martha. Thank you.

She leaves. Pause.

GALEN. So, tell me, Doctor, what do you feel? About what I've said?

VICTOR. Nothing. I'm just a doctor.

GALEN. A Doctor Faustus?

VICTOR. If you like. Not really.

GALEN. But you must have feelings. What do you feel about what the clinic does?

VICTOR. Well –

Pause.

I think that we're probably doing the right thing. For the country, I mean.

GALEN. Is that what you always think?

VICTOR. I suppose so.

Pause. Coughs again.

GALEN. I don't believe you, Doctor.

VICTOR. Why ever not?

GALEN. Because I can see it. You're a sensitive soul. You like wine and cheese. And you care for your maid. You notice the weather. You engage in conversation.

Pause.

And you're ill, aren't you? I can tell.

VICTOR. I'm dying, your reverence. Lung cancer. Self-diagnosed.

GALEN. I'm sorry to hear that. I will pray for you.

VICTOR. Thank you. I'm sure it will help.

Smiles wryly. Pause.

GALEN. So?

VICTOR. Yes?

GALEN. Well, what do you feel about what you're doing here? What does your heart tell you?

VICTOR. My heart?

GALEN. Your soul.

Pause.

VICTOR. Well, I don't know if this is what you'd call my soul speaking, but –

Pause.

GALEN. Yes?

VICTOR. I sometimes remember my mother.

GALEN. Your mother?

VICTOR. Yes, she died two years ago. Very old.

GALEN. My condolences.

VICTOR. Oh, she was born in 1848.

GALEN. Goodness, the year of revolutions.

VICTOR. And terribly frail. Ninety-one. Dementia. Incontinent.
In the last few years she didn't recognise me at all. Couldn't
look after herself. Needed continuous care.

GALEN. And?

VICTOR. Well, since you ask, she was like some of the
children here. Entirely vulnerable. And I'm not sure if her
life was worth –

Pause.

So that's what I feel. That's what my soul, as you call it,
says, when it speaks. Not often, but sometimes.

Pause.

And that's all I'm going to say on the matter.

GALEN. I see.

Pause.

Look, Doctor Franz, life is hard. We're born, we grow old
and we die. We work and we struggle. We do what we can to
make our lives bearable. Some of us, if granted the gift, work
for the common good. We fight against what we think is
wrong, and we support what is good. And when we die –

Pause as he looks at VICTOR.

When we die we're remembered for a few years by our
children – if we have them – and in the memory of our
friends and brethren if we don't, and that is all. I believe
that after death we're judged by our maker. I take it that you

don't share that faith. That is your right. But in every other respect we are the same. You and I. Your mother and these children in your care. Human life is indivisible. But those of us who are strong, who have power, who have access to power, well, we have a responsibility to those who don't. It's simple, really. Don't you see?

There is no reply.

As I'm sure you know, I despise the Soviet Union. I hate Communism with all my heart. I hate the lie on which it's built. And I hate its cruelty. But we're not much better, you know, we Germans. We too fail to respect human life. We too think that everything can be measured, weighed up, that every man has his price. We've forgotten that human life is sacred. We've forgotten what Christ meant when he said 'whatsoever you do to the least of these, you do unto me'. We've forgotten the things that matter.

Pause.

And that's why you must stop this killing. Because you're killing your brother and sister. You're killing your mother and father. You're killing yourself.

VICTOR (*coughs*). And what about animals?

GALEN. I beg your pardon?

VICTOR. Do you think we shouldn't kill animals?

GALEN. I fail to see the connection.

VICTOR. Well, explain to me, if you would, the difference between a dog, a sharp, sly, healthy hunting dog, let's say, and one of my patients. Or my mother, come to think of it. Think of the difference in abilities. Why should we protect one and not the other? Give me the dog any day. For company.

Pause.

What's your answer to that?

GALEN. Doctor, to live an ethical life one must develop a feeling for the sacred, one must have an understanding of God's law. Your rationality, your logic, your science only leads you into sin, don't you see?

VICTOR. Does it always?

GALEN. It does. It does. It is the sin of modernity. It rejects the
absolute. But God's great gift of life is sacred. That is all that
can be said.

VICTOR. I don't understand the word 'sacred', I'm afraid. It has
no place in my vocabulary.

GALEN. Then you must find your own reasons for living a good
life. You must, I tell you, you must.

Pause.

It's your duty. To yourself.

Pause.

And to the memory of your mother.

Pause.

And now I must go.

Stands.

Thank you for your hospitality.

VICTOR. I'll call the maid.

Goes and calls for MARTHA, *who quickly appears.*

Get the Bishop his coat, would you?

MARTHA. Of course.

*She leaves and returns moments later with his coat, scarf,
gloves, hat and helps him on with them.*

It's started to snow, your reverence.

GALEN. Yes, January. Fresh snow. New beginnings. So,
goodbye.

Shakes hands with VICTOR.

VICTOR. Martha, could you show Bishop von Galen the way
down to his car?

GALEN. Thank you, Doctor. Goodbye.

He starts to leaves with MARTHA. ERIC *enters.*

ERIC. Good evening, Bishop. Heil Hitler.

GALEN....?

He looks at VICTOR.

VICTOR. Herr Schmidt. My deputy.

GALEN. Ah yes, Schmidt. Good evening.

They stand stiffly. Don't shake hands.

ERIC. Did you have a useful meeting? Everything sorted?

GALEN. I beg your pardon?

ERIC. 'Suffer the little children to come unto me'? Is that what you've been talking about?

VICTOR. Herr Schmidt.

GALEN. Doctor Franz told me all about you.

ERIC. Did he?

GALEN. A fanatic, apparently.

ERIC. Excuse me?

GALEN. No?

Pause.

And what's your opinion?

ERIC. I beg your pardon.

GALEN. About what you're doing here.

VICTOR. Martha –

GALEN. This attack on children. Is that a good thing to do?

VICTOR. Martha –

GALEN. Well?

MARTHA. Doctor –

VICTOR (*sharply*). Leave, I said.

She leaves.

GALEN. Well?

ERIC. What?

GALEN. You heard me. This campaign of state-sponsored murder. Do you think it's the right thing to do? Do you think it's moral?

Pause.

Is this what your life has come to?

ERIC. Part of my life. Not all of it.

GALEN. I see. And how old are you?

ERIC. Twenty-three.

GALEN. And do you not remember the Sixth Commandment: 'Thou shalt not kill'?

ERIC. I remember it.

GALEN. And what's your response?

ERIC. Your reverence, with respect – or perhaps not? – I don't think you really understand what's happening here in Germany.

GALEN. I beg your pardon.

ERIC. The thing is, your reverence, your holiness or whatever we're meant to call you, you're not in charge any more. We've had enough of people like you. Clever people who think they know everything. Grand people who scrounge off the rest of us. We've had enough.

GALEN. How ridiculous.

ERIC. Don't you see: we're creating a new world here. We don't care about the past. We don't care about bishops with cathedrals and cardinals and popes. This is a new age, and everything has changed. Everything. We're building a new future.

GALEN. And what kind of a future is that going to be?

ERIC. A future where we can breathe. Where we have fresh air to breathe.

GALEN. How preposterous.

ERIC. Let me tell you something, Bishop. May I tell you
    something?

GALEN. Doctor Franz, please –

VICTOR. Herr Schmidt.

ERIC. I know what you've been telling the doctor, and I know
    about your letter to the paper. But, don't you see, there's no
    room for the kind of people you defend, the scroungers, the
    useless feeders. Not any more. These are hard times we're
    living in, as I'm sure you know, and we have new values.
    New priorities. There's no room for weakness, for failure.
    Not any more.

GALEN. I will pray for you. God's infinite mercy may stretch
    so far –

ERIC. I don't give a shit about God's infinite mercy.

VICTOR. Eric, please –

ERIC. It's just another lie. Let me tell you about these people
    here, these, these –

Pause.

GALEN. These children? Go on.

ERIC. I hate them. With their blind, dumb faces. Their drooling
    mouths. Their filthy clothes. Their piss and shit everywhere.
    It's disgusting.

Pause.

And let me tell you something else, Bishop. My old dad
worked on the railways. He was an engineer, wasn't he? Out
of Bremen. The docks, you know. And then the last war
came along and in the last moment – the very last moment –
we got beat. And when he came home from the front, he had
no legs and a stoved-in face. And every day of my life I had
to look at that face. Over my breakfast. Hands that didn't
work. A brain that didn't work.

Pause.

You see, his life had been ruined. Not by the people who shot at him. No, they were good Yankee boys: the land of the free. No, the people who smashed up his face were that lot who stayed at home and did nothing to help him. The people who betrayed him. The Jews. The Reds. And the queers.

Pause.

And priests like you, no doubt.

Pause.

What did my old dad fight for, eh? So people like you could drink his blood? Piss on his grave? Eat his poor broken body? It makes me sick.

Pause.

And, Bishop, I'll tell you something else.

GALEN. No threats, please.

ERIC. We have the power now. And we'll win.

VICTOR. Forgive him, Bishop, please –

GALEN. 'He knows not what he does'?

ERIC. I'm not joking.

GALEN. I pray for the Nazis too.

ERIC. I bet you do.

VICTOR. Your reverence, thank you for coming, and I apologise for –

GALEN. A pleasure. Most instructive.

Pause.

There is little more I can say to you. Or to your depraved friend here. You must find your own way through. But all I know is this: every time you persecute those who are less fortunate than you, God weeps. Every time you let one of these children be killed, you kill part of yourself. I will continue to write letters. And, soon, I will take this meeting as the subject of a sermon at the cathedral and let the world know what is happening here. I will continue to stand up for what is right. There is nothing else I can do. Goodnight, gentlemen.

He leaves.

Pause.

ERIC. Well?

VICTOR. Well what?

ERIC. The 'Lion of Münster', eh? Isn't that what he's called?

VICTOR. Apparently.

Pause.

ERIC. He got to you, didn't he?

VICTOR. Not really.

ERIC. Sure?

Pause.

VICTOR. Absolutely.

ERIC. Good.

Pause.

Because it's all bullshit, you know. You do know that don't you, Doctor? Religious bullshit. Just ignore it. It's all a lie, you know.

VICTOR. Yes.

Pause.

I'll ignore it.

ERIC. Good.

Pause.

It's bloody cold out there. We're going to be snowed in, I think.

VICTOR. You been out?

ERIC. I had a –

VICTOR. I see.

VICTOR *coughs and splutters*.

ERIC. That's bad that cough.

VICTOR. Hmm.

ERIC. Getting worse.

VICTOR. Maybe.

Pause.

Now look here, Eric –

ERIC. Yes?

Pause.

VICTOR. I've decided to postpone tomorrow's transport.

ERIC. What?

VICTOR. Just for a few days. To think things through.

ERIC. And what have you told Berlin?

VICTOR. Nothing, yet, I –

ERIC. Then I will. I'm sorry, Doctor, but –

VICTOR. It's up to you.

Pause.

ERIC. It'll make no difference, you know.

Pause.

It won't stop us, you know. It won't stop the programme.

VICTOR. I know. But I have to do something. I have to.

Pause.

ERIC. So the Bishop did get to you?

VICTOR. He did. And he has quite a following, you know. He could –

ERIC. Oh, don't be ridiculous. He can give a sermon or two, if he likes, but they'll arrest him and send him somewhere to calm down. The Führer's not going to put up with that kind of shit, you know. And anyway, nobody listens to bishops any more.

VICTOR. Martha does.

ERIC. How sweet.

VICTOR. She does. And there are thousands of people just like her, all over the place.

Pause.

And then there's Frau Pabst. What about Frau Pabst, eh?

ERIC. What about her?

VICTOR. What can be said to her?

ERIC. We did her a favour.

VICTOR. We all have mothers, Eric. I had a mother.

ERIC. But who's going to listen to them?

Pause.

And what about that mother who wrote to the Führer thanking him for putting her spastic son out of his misery? She was grateful. They all are, deep down. They hate their children when they're like that. It's just that some of them, well, they won't admit it.

VICTOR. Perhaps.

Pause.

I wouldn't know.

Pause.

ERIC. So, what now?

VICTOR. I told you.

ERIC. And are you going to do it?

VICTOR. I am.

ERIC. Well, that's your decision as Clinical Director. But you do know that it's a pointless gesture. The German people expect their doctors to support the people's interests. Not work against them.

Pause.

And you won't get another position. Your career will be over. You do understand that, don't you?

Pause.

So, they'll dismiss you and find someone who's prepared to fill the quotas. Exceed them, even.

VICTOR. Like you, no doubt.

Pause.

But at least I'll be able to sleep at night.

ERIC. So long as they let you.

Pause.

So, goodnight, Doctor. Hope you don't have bad dreams. And don't forget, Doctor: Heil Hitler.

VICTOR *is silent.*

Heil Hitler.

ERIC *gives a full Hitler salute and on his way out bumps into* MARTHA, *who's on her way in, very upset.*

MARTHA. Doctor, I need to talk to you.

ERIC. Oh, get out of my way, you stupid bitch.

He barges into her, and she falls to the floor, banging her head on the door.

You stupid fucking bitch.

He spits on her.

VICTOR. Eric –

ERIC. I'll do what I like. I'll do what I fucking well like. Goodnight.

ERIC *leaves.*

VICTOR. Martha, what happened – ?

MARTHA. He pushed me.

She's bleeding.

I banged my head on the –

VICTOR. Come here, come on, sit down.

MARTHA. He spat at me. And I'm bleeding, look.

VICTOR. Hang on a second. Calm down, calm down, it's just
a little –

*He tries to clean her up. But as the initial shock wears off,
she gets more and more emotional.*

MARTHA. What was all that about?

VICTOR. I'll have a word with him –

MARTHA. What did I do? What's the matter with him? Tell
me, Doctor.

VICTOR. I don't know. I just don't know.

MARTHA. He's like… He's like the ratcatcher or something.
He's – He's –

Pause.

And what's going on here anyway, Doctor? What did the
Bishop mean when he said that –

VICTOR. Martha, I –

MARTHA. – you were 'attacking children' here?

Pause.

What did he mean?

Pause.

Oh Doctor, I love my country. I love this job. But what's
happening here, eh? Please, tell me. What's happening?

VICTOR. It's all very complicated, Martha, you see –

MARTHA. And what was that you said to Frau Pabst about her son? And why did the Bishop say just now that it was evil?

VICTOR. Look, Martha, have some water.

MARTHA. What did he do wrong, that poor helpless boy? Why did he have to –

He gives her a drink.

Thank you.

Pause.

And Grete's in a terrible state too. She phoned me in the maid's room just now, she said she needs money for something important but she won't tell me what it is. I think she's pregnant and wants to get rid of it. I don't know what Herr Schmidt wants, he probably wants the – But what would the Bishop think, eh? We're Catholics. She can't –

VICTOR. And it's against the law, isn't it?

MARTHA. I know. I know.

Crosses herself. Pause.

Oh Doctor, I worry so much. About the children. Not just mine, but all of them. I know we're meant to look down on the ones here and say that they're useless. But I don't. I love them. I love every single one of them. I love my own children, of course, and I'm glad that they're not – But I love the ones here too. Even the stupid ones. Even the ones who can't do anything. Even the ones who just sit in their chairs dribbling.

Pause.

I used to be so scared of them. They seemed so different to me. As if they'd infect me with their illnesses. As if I'd become like one of them. And they *are* different. But they don't scare me any more. They're just children, aren't they? They're just children. All our children.

VICTOR. Just children. Yes.

Pause.

MARTHA. We need to help them, don't we? We need to look after them.

Pause.

Is this what we've come to? Is it?

Pause.

VICTOR (*coughs and splutters*). I don't know. I don't know anything any more. But, yes, you're right. Protect them. Keep them safe. Give them a better future. I've no idea how to do that, but, yes, that's what we have to do. We have to.

MARTHA. Good. I'm glad.

Pause.

You're leaving here, aren't you?

VICTOR. How did you know?

MARTHA. I just knew.

Pause.

VICTOR. Yes, I am.

MARTHA. And what will happen to you?

VICTOR. I don't know. They'll probably send me to a concentration camp, Martha. Or worse.

Pause.

But I have to do something.

Pause. She's crying.

Here, let me clean that. I am a doctor, you know.

He cleans off the blood and dabs antiseptic on to her face. It stings her. He's coughing as the lights fade. Schubert plays.

The End.

Other Titles in this Series

Mike Bartlett
BULL
GAME
AN INTERVENTION
KING CHARLES III
WILD

Howard Brenton
55 DAYS
#AIWW: THE ARREST OF AI WEIWEI
ANNE BOLEYN
BERLIN BERTIE
DANCES OF DEATH
DOCTOR SCROGGY'S WAR
DRAWING THE LINE
ETERNAL LOVE
FAUST – PARTS ONE & TWO *after* Goethe
LAWRENCE AFTER ARABIA
NEVER SO GOOD
PAUL
THE RAGGED TROUSERED
    PHILANTHROPISTS *after* Tressell

Jez Butterworth
THE FERRYMAN
JERUSALEM
JEZ BUTTERWORTH PLAYS: ONE
MOJO
THE NIGHT HERON
PARLOUR SONG
THE RIVER
THE WINTERLING

Caryl Churchill
BLUE HEART
CHURCHILL PLAYS: THREE
CHURCHILL PLAYS: FOUR
CHURCHILL: SHORTS
CLOUD NINE
DING DONG THE WICKED
A DREAM PLAY *after* Strindberg
DRUNK ENOUGH TO SAY
    I LOVE YOU?
ESCAPED ALONE
FAR AWAY
HERE WE GO
HOTEL
ICECREAM
LIGHT SHINING IN
    BUCKINGHAMSHIRE
LOVE AND INFORMATION
MAD FOREST
A NUMBER
PIGS AND DOGS
SEVEN JEWISH CHILDREN
THE SKRIKER
THIS IS A CHAIR
THYESTES *after* Seneca
TRAPS

David Haig
THE GOOD SAMARITAN
MY BOY JACK
PRESSURE

Lucy Kirkwood
BEAUTY AND THE BEAST
    with Katie Mitchell
BLOODY WIMMIN
THE CHILDREN
CHIMERICA
HEDDA *after* Ibsen
IT FELT EMPTY WHEN THE
    HEART WENT AT FIRST BUT
    IT IS ALRIGHT NOW
LUCY KIRKWOOD PLAYS: ONE
NSFW
TINDERBOX

Conor McPherson
DUBLIN CAROL
McPHERSON PLAYS: ONE
McPHERSON PLAYS: TWO
McPHERSON PLAYS: THREE
THE NEST *after* Franz Xaver Kroetz
THE NIGHT ALIVE
PORT AUTHORITY
THE SEAFARER
SHINING CITY
THE VEIL
THE WEIR

Diane Samuels
3 SISTERS ON HOPE STREET
    with Tracy-Ann Oberman
KINDERTRANSPORT
POPPY + GEORGE
THE TRUE LIFE FICTION OF
    MATA HARI

Steve Waters
THE CONTINGENCY PLAN
FAST LABOUR
IGNORANCE/JAHILIYYAH
LIMEHOUSE
LITTLE PLATOONS
TEMPLE
THE UNTHINKABLE
WORLD MUSIC

Carly Wijs
US/THEM

Nicholas Wright
CRESSIDA
HIS DARK MATERIALS
    after Pullman
THE LAST OF THE DUCHESS
LULU *after* Wedekind
MRS KLEIN
RATTIGAN'S NIJINSKY
REGENERATION
    after Pat Barker
THE REPORTER
THÉRÈSE RAQUIN *after* Zola
THREE SISTERS *after* Chekhov
TRAVELLING LIGHT
VINCENT IN BRIXTON
WRIGHT: FIVE PLAYS

A Nick Hern Book

All Our Children first published in Great Britain in 2017 as a paperback original by Nick Hern Books Limited, The Glasshouse, 49a Goldhawk Road, London W12 8QP, in association with Tara Finney Productions

Cover image: Rebecca Pitt

Designed and typeset by Nick Hern Books, London
Printed and bound in Great Britain by Mimeo Ltd, Huntingdon, Cambridgeshire PE29 6XX

A CIP catalogue record for this book is available from the British Library

ISBN 978 1 84842 669 6

Woodland
CARBON
www.woodlandcarbon.co.uk
NICK HERN BOOKS
Printed on Carbon Captured paper

www.nickhernbooks.co.uk

facebook.com/nickhernbooks

twitter.com/nickhernbooks